8th Avenue

7th Avenue

Broadway

6th Avenue

Bryant Park

37 · 38 · 39 · 40 · 41 · 42 · 43 · 44 · 45 · 46 · 47 · 48 · 49

• INDICATES THEATRES IN BOOK

•1 ABBEY'S

•2 CASINO

•3 PRINCESS

•4 NAZIMOVA'S 39TH STREET

•5 MAXINE ELLIOTT

•6 EMPIRE

7 NEDERLANDER

•8 BROADWAY (41ST STREET)

•9 COMEDY

•10 LEW M. FIELDS

•11 AMERICAN

•12 ELTINGE

•13 LIBERTY

•14 CANDLER

•15 NEW AMSTERDAM

•16 TIMES SQUARE

•17 REPUBLIC

•18 VICTORIA

•19 SELWYN

•20 FORD CENTER

•21 APOLLO

•22 LYRIC

•23 GEORGE M. COHAN

•24 HENRY MILLER'S

25 ST. JAMES

26 HELEN HAYES

•27 WEBER & FIELDS'

•28 HIPPODROME

29 MARTIN BECK

30 MAJESTIC (45TH STREET)

31 BROADHURST

32 SHUBERT

33 JOHN GOLDEN (45TH STREET)

34 ROYALE

35 PLYMOUTH

36 BOOTH

37 MINSKOFF

38 CRITERION CENTER

•39 OLYMPIA

•40 HUDSON

41 BELASCO

•42 KLAW

43 MUSIC BOX

•44 MOROSCO

•45 BIJOU

•46 ASTOR

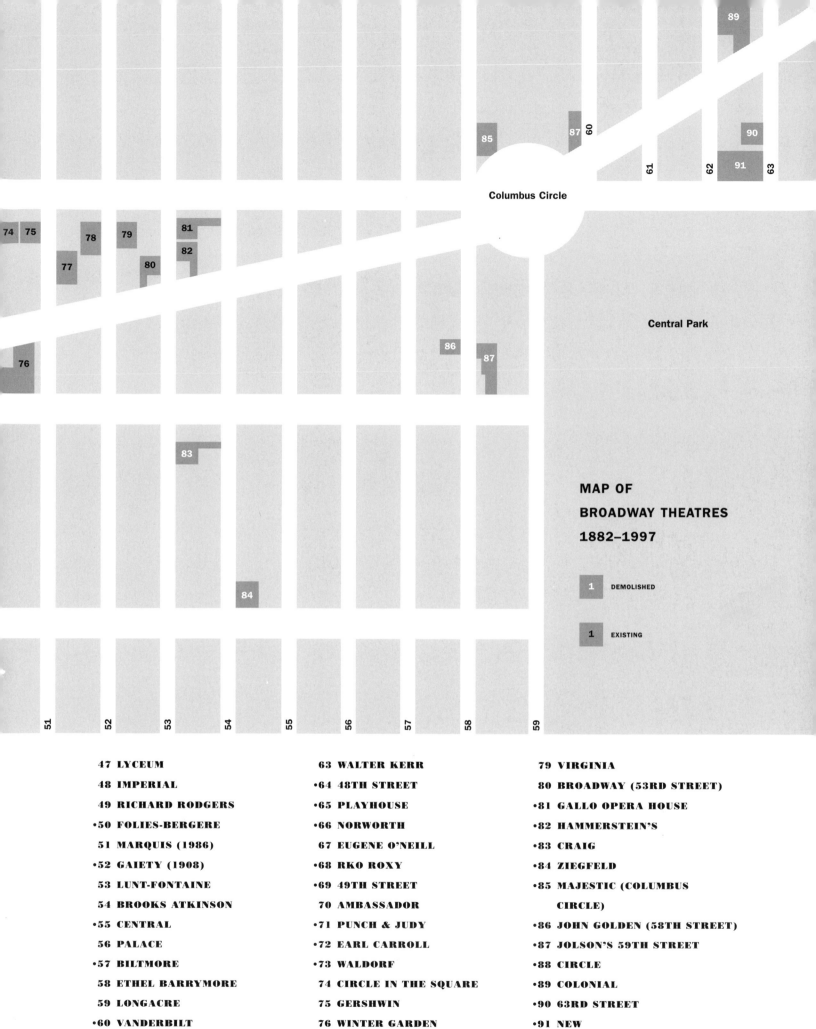

Columbus Circle

Central Park

**MAP OF
BROADWAY THEATRES
1882–1997**

| 1 | DEMOLISHED |

| 1 | EXISTING |

47 LYCEUM

48 IMPERIAL

49 RICHARD RODGERS

•50 FOLIES-BERGERE

51 MARQUIS (1986)

•52 GAIETY (1908)

53 LUNT-FONTAINE

54 BROOKS ATKINSON

•55 CENTRAL

56 PALACE

•57 BILTMORE

58 ETHEL BARRYMORE

59 LONGACRE

•60 VANDERBILT

61 CORT

•62 EDYTH TOTTEN

63 WALTER KERR

•64 48TH STREET

•65 PLAYHOUSE

•66 NORWORTH

67 EUGENE O'NEILL

•68 RKO ROXY

•69 49TH STREET

70 AMBASSADOR

•71 PUNCH & JUDY

•72 EARL CARROLL

•73 WALDORF

74 CIRCLE IN THE SQUARE

75 GERSHWIN

76 WINTER GARDEN

•77 HOLLYWOOD

78 NEIL SIMON

79 VIRGINIA

80 BROADWAY (53RD STREET)

•81 GALLO OPERA HOUSE

•82 HAMMERSTEIN'S

•83 CRAIG

•84 ZIEGFELD

•85 MAJESTIC (COLUMBUS
   CIRCLE)

•86 JOHN GOLDEN (58TH STREET)

•87 JOLSON'S 59TH STREET

•88 CIRCLE

•89 COLONIAL

•90 63RD STREET

•91 NEW

LOST BROADWAY THEATRES

NICHOLAS VAN HOOGSTRATEN

WITH ADDITIONAL PHOTOGRAPHY BY
JOCK POTTLE AND MAGGIE HOPP

REVISED EDITION

FULLY UPDATED AND EXPANDED

PRINCETON ARCHITECTURAL PRESS

Published by:
Princeton Architectural Press
37 East Seventh Street
New York, NY 10003

01 00 99 98   5 4 3 2   First Revised Edition

Editors, first edition:
Stephanie Lew and Elizabeth Short

Editor, revised edition:
Mark Lamster

Cover design:
Sara E. Stemen

Book design:
J. Abbott Miller

Layout, revised edition:
Mark Lamster

Special thanks to: Gina Bell, Caroline Green, Clare Jacobson, Therese Kelly, Annie Nitschke, and
Sara E. Stemen of Princeton Architectural Press—Kevin C. Lippert, publisher.

Printed and bound in Canada

ISBN 1-56898-116-3

Library of Congress Cataloging-in-Publication Data for this title is available from the publisher.

For a free catalog of books published by Princeton Architectural Press, call toll free 1.800.722.6657
or visit www.papress.com on the World Wide Web.

Front cover:
Vanderbilt Theatre, 1918. Photo courtesy the Harry Ransom Humanities
Reseach Center, the University of Texas at Austin.

Back cover:
Left: Hammerstein Theatre lantern, 1990. Photo courtesy Jock Pottle.
Right: Earl Carroll Theatre interior, 1988. Photo courtesy Jock Pottle.

FOR MY PARENTS

ACKNOWLEDGMENTS

This book would not have been possible without the encouragement, enthusiasm, and dedication of dozens of people and their organizations. At the Rockefeller Development Corporation, John Burnett, John Hessmer, and Jim Reed generously allowed me to explore the Earl Carroll Theatre building. My discoveries there provided the inspiration for this project. Their interest was beyond the call of duty and without it *Lost Broadway Theatres* would never have been started. The majority of illustrations in this book come from museums, libraries, and private collections nationwide. The experts who came to my aid during my bursts of research did so with unfailing professionalism, devotion, and humor.

The Booth-Hampden Library - Ray Wemblinger
George Mason University - Ruth Kearns
Harvard Theatre Collection - Jeanne T. Newlin
The Museum of the City of New York - Katherine Mets
The New York Historical Society - Dale Neighbors, Patricia Paladines
The New York Public Library - Bob Taylor and the entire staff of curators, librarians, and pages at the Billy Rose Theatre Arts Collection at the Lincoln Center branch.
University of Texas at Austin - Prentiss Moore
The Old York Library - Seymour Durst
The Shubert Archives - Maryann Chach, Reagan Fletcher, Mark Swartz
Wisconsin Center for Film and Television - Reg Shrader

A special note of appreciation must also go to three individuals whose contributions made this project complete. Peggy Elson made available for study the papers, plans, and photographs of her father, theatre architect Herbert J. Krapp. The images from Terry Helgesen's unique and varied collection reflect his life-long interest in theatres. Information gathered by author William Morrison for his own upcoming study of Broadway theatres filled many gaps in my research. I am thankful for their considerable generosity. Companies with an active interest in theatre buildings gave me invaluable cooperation and access to their properties. For their trust and support I am grateful to Douglas Durst, Seymour Durst, and Will Dailey of The Durst Organization, Toney Edwards of T.E. Management, Kathy Raitt and Peter Russell at The Nederlander Organization, Lon Siegel at First Winthrop Corporation, and Kent Swig, Pamela Noyes, and Barbara Reierson at The Macklowe Organization. Equity News, the monthly newsletter of Actor's Equity Association, graciously printed two requests for material for this book. Many thanks to the dozens of people who responded, particularly Marcia Worth, Ruth Cameron, Rae Maquire, Howard Lindsay II, B.J. Rogers, Richard Graham,

ACKNOWLEDGMENTS

Patrick Watkins, Bob Burland, and Guy Little. Also making valuable contributions were Violet Carlson, Julie Harris, Michael Miller, Don Costello, Betty Tiffany, William Hammerstein, W. J. Dailey, and Curt Haggedorn and Brian Kaman of Save the Theatres, Inc.

Anyone with any affection for the great old theatres of Broadway owes a debt of gratitude to Cora Cahan and the staff of The New 42nd Street Inc., who continue to play a vital part in the mammoth task of rescuing two city blocks from oblivion. Their unqualified success benefits every person who strolls down 42nd Street and has made the updating of this book necessary.

At Princeton Architectural Press, Kevin Lippert and Elizabeth Short gave me constant, enthusiastic support from the very beginning, with editors Stephanie Lew and Mark Lamster offering guidance and objectivity. Sara Stemen provided an elegant cover for the revised edition. Behind the camera, Jock Pottle and Maggie Hopp risked bruised knees and sprained necks crawling above ceilings, climbing rotted stairs, and crouching in tight corners to capture the perfect views of the old theatres they photographed. Thanks to them, assistant Chris Gray, and printers Susan Daboil and Chuck Kelton.

And finally, for three years I imposed on friends and family for help, encouragement, and perspective. Without Mary Helen Curtis, Ellen Eisenberg, Anne, Wayne, and Bill Fredericks, Bruce and Cathy Frumerman, Paul and Julie Harman, Art Hyman, Jaki Keuch, Ellen Kornblum, Lori Oddino, Mary Orgon, and John and Rosemary Raitt, writing this book would have been twice as difficult and half as much fun. A heartfelt thanks to all for helping to make it happen.

TABLE OF CONTENTS

	Map of Broadway	2
	Acknowledgments	8
	Introduction	13
	Theatres	
1882	Casino	15
1888	Broadway	19
1893	Empire	23
	American	29
	Abbey's	33
1895	Olympia	37
1899	Victoria	41
1900	Republic	45
1901	Circle	53
1903	Majestic	57
	Lyric	61
	Hudson	67
	New Amsterdam	73
1904	Liberty	83
	Lew M. Fields	87
1905	Colonial	91
	Hippodrome	95
1906	Astor	101
1908	Gaiety	105
	Maxine Elliott's	109
1909	Comedy	113
	New	117
	63rd Street	123
1910	Nazimova's	127
1911	George M. Cohan	129
	Playhouse	135
	Folies-Bergere	137
1912	48th Street	143
	Eltinge	147
1913	Weber & Fields'	151
	Princess	155
1914	Candler	159
	Punch & Judy	163
1917	Morosco	167
	Bijou	171
1918	Norworth	175
	Vanderbilt	177
	Henry Miller's	179
	Central	183
	Selwyn	187
1920	Times Square	191
	Apollo	195
1921	Klaw	199
	Jolson's	203
	49th Street	207
1923	Earl Carroll	209
1926	Edyth Totten	219
	Waldorf	221
1927	John Golden	223
	Ziegfeld	227
	Gallo	231
	Hammerstein's	237
1928	Craig	243
1932	RKO Roxy	247
	Addendum: Theatres added to the revised edition	
1925	Biltmore	251
1930	Hollywood	253
	Appendix of drawings, plans, & sections	254
	Bibliography	284
	Index	286
	Epilogue	288

INTRODUCTION

Originally located at the lower end of Manhattan, New York City's theatre district moved steadily northward throughout the nineteenth century. New forms of transportation brought the city's growing population to theatres at Union Square, Madison Square, Herald Square, and finally, at the end of the century, Longacre Square, which had become a hub for horsecar and train lines. In 1904 the subway system made the renamed Times Square even more accessible with a main stop at 42nd Street and Broadway.

Concurrent to the development of Times Square was the growing importance of New York as the center of America's theatre business. Hundreds of playhouses throughout the country were supplied with shows "direct from New York" by a number of producing firms. Fierce competition between the two largest, Klaw & Erlanger's Theatrical Syndicate and the Shuberts, forced each firm to build theatres for its own exclusive use. As the demand for new shows skyrocketed, so did the number of new theatres.

Beginning with the Casino in 1882 and ending fifty years later with the Hollywood in 1932, the construction of nearly ninety theatres in the blocks between Times Square and Columbus Circle gave the area the largest concentration of playhouses in the world. The stock market crash of 1929 and the depression that it signaled, however, sharply reduced the demand for theatre. Some houses converted to showing movies, some became radio (and later television) studios, others nightclubs. Often, they were demolished as their land and tax values soared. Today, only thirty-eight playhouses remain devoted to the live stage. The following fifty-six chapters take a look back at the buildings, people, and stories that contributed so much to the legend of Broadway. Most of these theatres are gone forever. But perhaps a few, with a little ingenuity and a lot of capital, will be restored to a tradition that turned a mile-long part of midtown Manhattan into the Great White Way.

CASINO

6TH BIG MONTH
YOU MUST SEE
EXPERIENCE
THE MOST WONDERFUL
PLAY IN
NEW YORK

NEIL TERRY

Casino
YOU MUST SEE
EXPERIENCE

HOTEL NORMANDIE

Casino Theatre Bway & 39 St.
Copyright 1913 by Irving Underhill NY

CASINO THEATRE

BROADWAY AT 39TH STREET KIMBALL & WISEDELL, 1882

When the Casino Theatre opened in 1882 it was farther uptown than any of the city's ten other legitimate playhouses. Built by producer Rudolph Aronson and financed by the likes of the Morgans, Tiffanys, Goulds, Vanderbilts, and Roosevelts, the project was known as "Aronson's Folly." The Casino, it was said, was simply too far removed from the theatre district (which at that time stretched nine blocks from Union Square to 23rd Street) to be successful. Based on the opening night, the Broadway gossips appeared to be right. Labor disputes and shortages of building materials had already delayed the premiere for six weeks by the time production contracts forced Aronson to open the Casino on 21 October. The show, Johann Strauss' operetta The Queen's Lace Handkerchief, was in good shape. The theatre, however, was not. With roughly two months of construction still needed, the interior was a shambles. Unbleached muslin covered large gaps in the walls and acted as room partitions. Paper substituted for glass in the unfinished windows and construction debris was littered throughout the building. As the unseasonably cold autumn air whistled through the auditorium it became clear that the heating system was incomplete. So was the roof. Soon after the curtain went up a heavy rainstorm started and the temporary canvas roof began to leak. The patrons who remained in their seats for the entire show did so under open umbrellas.

After one week Aronson sent the operetta out on the road and returned the Casino to the construction crews. When the show came back to the house on 30 December to continue its run, the Casino had been transformed into a gold, silver, and bronze beauty. Considered by some to be the finest example of Moorish architecture outside of Spain, its terra-cotta exterior was dominated by a seven-story round tower at the corner. Two flights of stairs led from the lobby to both a cafe and to the 1,300-seat auditorium. The plaster walls, moulded into a myriad of ornamental forms, were painted in rich metallic colors. Studded with paste jewels, the blue, brown, and gold velvets of the heavily-fringed house curtain also carried out the Moorish theme. Above the auditorium was the world's first roof garden. Ringed with brightly-colored electric lights, patrons were entertained while enjoying the cooling breezes of summer evenings and unobstructed views of the growing city. Light operas and operettas were strictly the fare at the Casino for the decade Aronson managed it. He brought some of the theatre's biggest stars to the house, including Lillian Russell, David Warfield, Marie Dressler, and Edna Wallace Hopper. He also mounted the Casino's longest run, the 571-performances of a long-forgotten British operetta called *Erminie*. The theatre's stockholders lost faith in Aronson, however, when he changed the theatre's policy to one of polite vaudeville in 1892. It flopped, and the following year control of the Casino passed to the theatrical firm of Canary & Lederer. For the first eight years, audience response to their productions was modest. But in 1900 they presented a musical that had the town talking for years.

LEFT : The Casino Theatre at the corner of Broadway and 39th Street in 1915. The Knickerbocker, formerly Abbey's Theatre, is next door. (YL)

ABOVE : The Casino's original interior before it was destroyed by fire in 1905. (MCNY)

The story of *Florodora,* which had to do with love, romance, and perfume in the Phillipines, was incidental to its popularity. One song, "Tell Me, Pretty Maiden," and the real-life escapades of the six maidens themselves kept *Florodora* in the papers for most of its 505-performance run. One of the "Florodora Girls" was secretly married to a nephew of Andrew Carnegie. When he unexpectedly died opening night, she became the richest chorus girl in the world. The five other chorines didn't do too badly either. They were courted by society's most eligible bachelors, and within six months each one had married a millionaire.

In 1903, after much litigation, Sam and Lee Shubert took over the lease of the Casino. It was their second theatre in New York City. Two years later, however, while presenting *Lady Teazle,* the first musical to carry the credit "The Messrs. Shubert present," they nearly lost the Casino in a devastating fire. Starting on the balcony level on a cold February morning, the fire quickly spread through much of the interior and into the neighboring cafe. It took an hour and a half to put out the blaze, a feat made more difficult by frozen water pumps. When the smoke had cleared, it was obvious the theatre would have to be rebuilt. The reconstructed Casino opened in November 1905 with another musical hit. *The Earl and the Girl* starred comic Eddie Foy and featured in its score a song by 20-year old Jerome Kern. "How'd You Like To Spoon With Me?" became Kern's first commercial hit. For the next twenty-five years the Shubert brothers kept the Casino stage occupied with their musicals. *Sally, Irene, and Mary; The Vagabond King;* and *The Desert Song* were three of the theatre's more popular attractions.

CASINO THEATRE

By 1930 the theatre, which had pioneered the move uptown forty-eight years earlier, had become the farthest downtown house still devoted to the stage. Over eighty legitimate theatres were in operation north of the Casino in a district that stretched beyond Columbus Circle. Following a performance of *Faust* by the American Opera Company, the Casino closed its doors forever. In February, the theatre was demolished to make way for thirty stories of workshops for the expanding garment district.

BELOW : The 1905 fire. (NYHS)

LEFT : Detail of the Casino's orchestra boxes. (MCNY)

BELOW : View of the rebuilt auditorium, 1917. (SA)

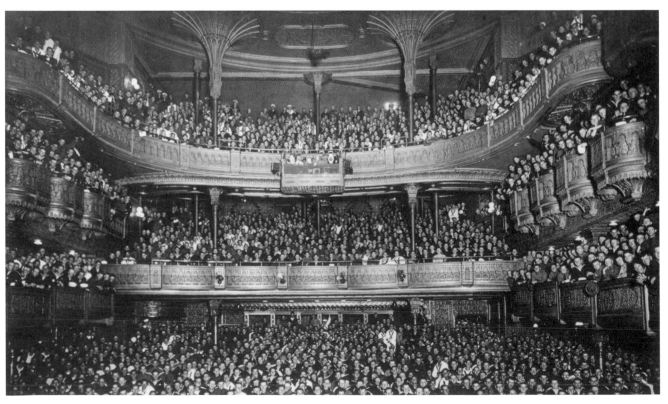

BROADWAY THEATRE

BROADWAY AT 41ST STREET   J.B. MCELFATRICK, 1888

One hundred years ago the corner of Broadway and 41st Street was not considered a viable location for a legitimate theatre. After all, the concert hall which occupied the site's five-story brick and brownstone building had failed under two different managements; even the skating rink subsequently built into the space met its demise after a brief burst of popularity. Nobody, the experts agreed, would travel so far uptown to be entertained.   At first James Bailey thought differently. A circus manager and former partner of P.T. Barnum, Bailey acquired the old Cosmopolitan Skating Rink, gutted the entire structure, and hired architect J.B. McElfatrick to design its conversion into a first-class theatre called the Broadway. The experts laughed, and this time maybe Bailey heard them. He sold his interest in the Broadway before the workmen were done, leaving new managers Frank Sanger, T.H. French, and Elliot Zborowski to open the house.   The Broadway Theatre was large even by modern standards, seating 1,800 and providing room for 500 standees. Its Persian style of decoration was unique among the city's European-influenced houses. Antique copper and glass chandeliers cast a soft glow over the Indian yellows, reds, and blues of the lobby walls and tapestries. The Eastern flavor continued into the auditorium, where the double tiers of proscenium boxes took the form of Iranian booths illuminated by swinging Persian lamps and separated from each other by large brass grills. Both of the Broadway's balconies abandoned the conventional horseshoe design in favor of a flatter curve, an innovation that greatly improved the sightlines of the side seats. Electric lights were used in the theatre for decoration as well as illumination; the tiny lights concealed in the sounding board and balcony fronts subdued the overall appearance of the colorful auditorium.   Nine days after *La Tosca* opened the Broadway on 3 March the famous blizzard of '88 devastated the city and closed 17 of its 25 theatres. The Broadway weathered the storm, but *La Tosca* did not. It was gone before the snow melted. The Broadway's first hit came that December. *Little Lord Fauntleroy* toured the country for years after its four-month run in New York. In 1889 audiences flocked to see Edwin Booth and Helene Modjeska in an eight-week season of classical repertory. The following year socialite Mrs. Leslie Carter made her stage debut in *The Ugly Duckling,* and in 1891 Edwin Booth returned in *Hamlet.* It was Booth's final appearance on a New York stage.   The Broadway continued to flourish at its uptown location. The original production of *Ben-Hur* was on view when the country entered into the new century. The adaptation of Lew Wallace's novel was one of the theatre's biggest employers, using a crew of 60 and a cast of 261 to present the spectacle to thrilled audiences for nearly six months. In 1903 Sir Henry Irving gave his final New York performance on the Broadway's stage. It was followed by *Utopia Limited,* a Gilbert and Sullivan collaboration.

BROADWAY THEATRE

The next decade saw appearances by Weber & Fields, Nora Bayes, Lillian Russell, Vernon Castle, and child actress Helen Hayes. In 1913, following the failure of John Philip Sousa's operetta *The American Maid,* the Broadway was converted into a film and vaudeville house. It remained as such until 2 January 1929 when the vaudeville *Broadway Fever* played one last time. After it closed, the 41-year old Broadway Theatre was demolished.

ABOVE : Broadway interior, 1888. (TH)

BELOW : Broadway Theatre, at the southwest corner of Broadway and 41st Street, in 1888. (HC)

LEFT : The Broadway as a movie theatre, 1915. (MCNY)

Byron N.Y.

EMPIRE THEATRE

1430 Broadway at 40th Street   J.B. McElfatrick, 1893

In the early 1890s, rich from the success of his first drama, producer Charles Frohman searched for a site for a new theatre he wanted to build. He focused on Herald Square until Al Hayman, a friend and colleague (and owner of a vacant lot at Broadway and 40th Street), told him that "everything theatrical is moving uptown." Frohman and his partner, William Harris, decided it was as good a place as any and gave Hayman the go-ahead to build the playhouse that became Broadway's favorite.

What made the Empire stand out from all the other theatres of Broadway was its simple, splendid hospitality. From the very first night in 1893 the Empire was in a class by itself. Patrons were welcomed at the narrow Broadway entrance by ticket-takers in full evening dress and silk hats. Beyond them were two expansive lobbies, allowing ample room for first-nighters to see and be seen. Around the corner on 40th Street were entrances to the second balcony and the stage. The 1,099-seat auditorium, considered to be the finest of the day, was handsomely decorated in tones of red, terra-cotta, cream, and dull green. Even the placement of the new electric lights was considered "most happy" by local critics.

Frohman opened his theatre with David Belasco's *The Girl I Left Behind Me,* the first of many popular and critical successes. The producer soon established a stock company of stars, including Maude Adams, William Gillette, and John Drew. His niece, Ethel Barrymore, appeared in *The Little Minister* in 1896. Six years later, Lionel Barrymore followed his sister on to the Empire stage in *The Mummy and the Humming Bird.*

When the house was ten years old, Frohman gutted the auditorium and lobbies and remodeled both in the rich style of Louis XIV. The outer lobby, modestly redone in light gray Caen stone, gave access to the larger second foyer through a trio of archways. The inner lobby doubled as a gallery for original oil paintings of the stars who played the Empire, a gallery that continued to grow in size for the next fifty years. The setting for these portraits rivaled the richness of the finest museums of the world. The new light red walls had panels of silk brocade divided by gold pilasters. The cornices and ornamentation were also gold, as was the barrel vault ceiling, which featured 18th century French murals. A thick red carpet completed the luxurious effect.

Dull gold was the predominant color of the new auditorium. Its rich luster decorated the balconies, boxes, ceiling, and proscenium, above which were painted murals matching those in the main lobby. The walls, carpets, and draperies of the rococo interior were deep red.

Critics were ecstatic over the new Empire. "It is not too much to say that this room is one of the most consistent, most appropriate, and cleverest pieces of interior decoration in this country," wrote *Architectural Record.* "No better example could be desired of the proper way to translate a classic style into a sufficiently modern equivalent." Audiences also appreciated the special qualities of the theatre. One fan of the Empire (and apparent anthropomorphist) sent a letter to *The New York Times* claiming "it was always an experience merely to walk into the theatre; the walls seemed to breathe and murmur, and there was something almost human even about the carpets."

LEFT : The original interior of the Empire Theatre, 1895. (MCNY)

ABOVE : The southeast corner of Broadway and 40th Street, 1895. (MCNY)

For the next dozen years Frohman and his stars flourished at the Empire. Sarah Bernhardt, Helen Hayes, Billie Burke, and the Barrymores kept the house packed. John Drew appeared in thirty productions, Maude Adams in twenty-one. During this period the premiere production of English writer J.M. Barrie's *Peter Pan*, starring Adams, was a runaway hit, prompting Frohman to make occasional trips to London in search of other plays. In 1915 he accepted an invitation from Barrie and sailed to England on the Lusitania. Off the coast of Ireland the ship was torpedoed by a German U-boat. Frohman perished in the disaster. Although its founder was gone, the Empire continued to be one of Broadway's most popular theatres. Control of the playhouse reverted to the family of Al Hayman, the man who actually built it. During the thirty-one years it remained in the Hayman family, a parade of stars including Lillian Gish, Basil Rathbone, Cornelia Otis Skinner, Ethel Waters, Leslie Howard, and Gertrude Lawrence graced its stage, and *Life With Father* made theatre history by playing without interruption for eight years. In 1948 the theatre was acquired by the Astor estate, which planned to one day develop the property. Five years later, upon the Empire's sixtieth anniversary, it was announced that the theatre's 279th and current tenant, *The Time of the Cuckoo,* would be its last. The news was met with a combination of sadness and resignation, the outcry checked by an unspoken understanding of the inevitability of progress. Other theatres would try to take its place, but theatre people would miss the Empire as they would an old friend. "Somehow," wrote Helen Hayes, "it doesn't seem believable to realize that next year we will walk down Broadway and find the corner of 40th Street an empty pit into which steamshovels and bulldozers are biting." Two weeks before demolition began an elaborate farewell was staged at the playhouse. *Highlights of the Empire* featured just that, the best from sixty years of Broadway comedies, dramas, and classics. Scenes from a dozen shows were presented, including one from the Empire's first, *The Girl I Left Behind Me,* with Edna Wallace Hopper recreating her original role in the 1893 comedy.

ABOVE : The Empire lost its Victorian flair when the entire theatre was renovated in 1903. This view of the auditorium dates from 1947. (WISC)

Following the final performance of *The Time of the Cuckoo,* the curtain remained up as the cast and audience stood and sang "Auld Lang Syne." Then, as the actors left the stage and cleaned out their dressing rooms, the audience cleaned out the rest of the building. They removed seat covers,

ABOVE : Empire orchestra section, 1947. (WISC)

light fixtures, and even plumbing in their frenzy to acquire a souvenir of the Empire. In the following days rows of seats went to actors, curtains and stage equipment were shipped to the Barter Theatre in Virginia, and plaster ram and Cupid heads from the lobby went to fans who had missed out on the seat covers.

The wrecker's ball took more than a beautiful old playhouse in 1953; its first swing signaled the end of an era. Of the scores of theatres that lined Union and Herald Squares, Broadway and the side streets south of 41st, the Empire was the last one still devoted to the legitmate stage. When it came down a two hundred year-old chapter in the history of New York theatre was finished.

Nearly forty years later, the Empire is still remembered fondly by the performers who played there. Julie Harris, who starred at the Empire in *I Am A Camera* and *The Member of the Wedding,* reminisced about the playhouse: "There was something special about acting on the Empire stage, knowing you had to reach the last row in the second balcony. The Victorian splendor gave such a sense of history, knowing the theatre greats had been on that stage . . . it was a glorious theatre—beautiful wood, damask silk walls, great theatre portraits. A tragedy that we lost it."

ABOVE : Auditorium ceiling, 1947. (WISC)

RIGHT : Empire lobby, 1947. (TH)

AMERICAN THEATRE

42ND STREET AND 8TH AVENUE   CHARLES C. HAIGHT, 1893

Imagine West 42nd Street seven years before the start of the twentieth century. It was the main thoroughfare of a primarily residential neighborhood. There were no stores, no streetcars or subways, not even any streetlights; the darkness was broken only by light from a local bar or parlor of a brownstone. It was in this undeveloped and un-welcoming neighborhood that a new era in theatre history would begin. Prior to the construction of the American Theatre in 1893, all major places of entertainment in Manhattan were located south of 42nd Street. Theatres flourished in Herald Square, Union Square, and Irving Place. But the area that would become known the world over as The Great White Way was little more than a collection of apartments, churches, general stores, and stables. While the wags downtown considered anything north of 40th Street to be the sticks, theatre manager and investor T. Henry French viewed this area as a land of opportunity. French, the son and partner of play publisher Samuel French, envisioned the American Theatre as a venue for melodramas controlled by his family's firm. For this purpose he built the third largest theatre in the city, and what would be the largest theatre on 42nd Street. Covering over half an acre of land, the American Theatre could be entered from three different streets. From the main entrance on 41st Street, patrons had access to all levels of the theatre. Two additional lobbies, on 42nd Street and on 8th Avenue, were designed for the exclusive use of the carriage trade and pedestrians, respectively. Over 2,100 spectators, including 200 standees, could fit in the orchestra, balcony, and gallery sections of the red and gold auditorium. The top of the proscenium was painted with a huge mural described by the New York Herald as representing "the daughters of Eve in some sort of function." Gilded gargoyles peered out from perches on top of the side walls. The gold dome which crowned the auditorium was fifty-seven feet in diameter. For the night owls in the audience, an open-air roof garden on top of the theatre offered a variety of entertainment each summer night immediately following the show downstairs. Electric lights, still considered a novelty, were used throughout the American, which was also the first theatre to whisk patrons to their balcony or roof garden seats in elevators. The theatre opened on 22 May 1893 with a tremendous success. Patrons from all over the city were lured to the American by the racetrack spectacle *The Prodigal Daughter,* which featured ten horses running diagonally across the stage in the first (and quite possibly only) steeplechase ever presented live on Broadway. More epics from the French catalogue followed, including *The Voyage of Suzette* with Maxine Elliott and Harry Davenport, but they never matched the success of the American's initial offering. In 1897 French lost the theatre through foreclosure, and the new management instituted a policy of light opera. Five years later the theatre changed policies once again, and the first of two seasons of the newly-formed American Stock Company was presented on its stage. Repertory drama failed, however, as did the

ABOVE : The 41st Street facade of the American. The stage occupies the right side of the building. (WB)

efforts of producers Klaw and Erlanger to make the house part of their theatrical syndicate. In 1908 booking agent William Morris leased and renovated the theatre, renamed it the American Music Hall, and kept it open with two-a-day vaudeville. The following summer the American Roof Garden reopened with a similar policy after having been rebuilt by theatre architect Thomas Lamb. In place of the old garden, a two-story theatre complete with balcony, boxes, and 1,400 seats was erected, surrounded by a promenade which took advantage of the American's three-street frontage. For the next twenty years, first under Morris

BELOW : View of the American's original open-air roof garden, looking southeast towards 41st Street, c. 1900. (MCNY)

and then, after 1912, under the direction of Marcus Loew, over six thousand vaudeville fans a day could be entertained in the two auditoriums of the American Theatre building.

Loew's death in 1927 marked the beginning of the end for the American Theatre. When Loew's, Incorporated withdrew from the American in 1929, both auditoriums closed. Developers announced plans to raze the theatre and construct in its place a thirty-story office building, but funding was lost in the stock market crash. Subsequently, a burlesque company leased the house and presented comics and strippers for the next year. On December 8, 1930 a fire started in the theatre after the final performance of the night. By the time the first alarm sounded, the fire had spread throughout the auditorium. The American Theatre would never reopen. The Eighth Avenue side of the building, untouched by the fire, was converted into bachelor apartments. Finally, eighteen months after the American Theatre burned, the entire structure was torn down. A traveling circus pitched its tent on the theatre site in 1933, and later a one-story "tax-payer" was constructed there. In 1997, all that remains on the site of the American Theatre is a parking lot.

ABOVE : The American Theatre's 42nd Street entrance shortly after its 1893 opening. (MCNY)

ABOVE : American Theatre foyer. Doors at left lead to the auditorium; balcony stairs and exit to 41st Street are straight ahead. (TX)

LEFT : In 1909 Thomas W. Lamb rebuilt the roof garden into a fourteen-hundred-seat enclosed theatre complete with balcony, boxes, and two open-air promenades. The new roof theatre had an "Adirondack lodge" atmosphere created by false tree trunks and leafy foliage decorations. (AB)

ABBEY'S THEATRE

1396 BROADWAY AT 38TH STREET CARRERE & HASTINGS, 1893

Producer and theatre manager Henry Abbey's uptown playhouse was part of a six-story office structure of limestone, buff brick, and granite. The entrance to the Italian Renaissance playhouse was through a two-story arch leading into a marble and onyx vestibule complete with fireplace, carved mahogany trimmings and wainscoting, and solid bronze doors. The auditorium, which could accommodate 1,500, had two deep balconies and six stage boxes decorated with elaborate metal railings. Sea green, white, and gold were the primary colors of the interior, carpets, and upholstery. Caught right in the middle of the transition from gas to electricity, Abbey used both to light the opalescent glass and brass globes that illuminated his theatre. The Abbey opened in grand style on 8 November 1893 as British star Sir Henry Irving made his fourth New York appearance with his repertory company, which included Ellen Terry. Beckett premiered the six-week engagement of several plays from Irving's list of hits. The Abbey quickly became a favorite of some of the era's biggest stars. Lillian Russell appeared twice the following season, and Irving and Terry returned during the Abbey's third year. Then, after managing his new playhouse for only three years, Henry Abbey died. Al Hayman, co-owner of the Empire Theatre, took over Abbey's in 1896 with partners Charles Frohman, Marc Klaw and Abe Erlanger. They renamed it the Knickerbocker and booked appearances by Sir Herbert Beerbohm, Maurice Barrymore (father of the soon-to-be famous siblings), Maxine Elliott, and the second return of Irving and Terry. Their sold-out three-week visit grossed $80,000 (that's 1899 dollars) thanks to the high demand of ticket speculators. The first season of the new century began with Maude Adams in *L'Aiglon,* and continued in following seasons with *Quality Street* (also with Adams), William Gillette in *Sherlock Holmes,* and Eddie Foy in *Mr. Bluebeard.* E.H. Southern and Julia Marlowe began a long acting partnership when they co-starred in *Romeo and Juliet* in 1904. Each reportedly earned a record weekly salary of $2,500. When *The Red Mill* played the Knickerbocker in 1906, producer Charles Dillingham erected a huge windmill outside the house to advertise the musical running inside. The display earned a minor place in Broadway history as the street's first moving electric sign and helped the show set the house record run of 40 weeks. George M. Cohan turned up in *The Yankee Prince* in 1908, Maude Adams returned three years later in *Chantecler,* and Douglas Fairbanks played in *The New Henrietta* in 1913. After Frohman's tragic death on the Lusitania in 1915, Abe Erlanger brought in Charles Dillingham as a new partner. Under their management the Knickerbocker presented George Arliss as *Disraeli* and Clifton Webb in the 34-week hit *Listen, Lester* in 1918. The theatre continued to present moderately successful shows throughout the next decade. These included Rodgers and Hart's 286-performance musical *Dearest Enemy* in 1925 and Kate Smith in the 1926 hit *Honeymoon Lane,* which played 317 times. When the house opened in 1893 only the Casino and the Broadway were further uptown. Thirty-seven years later the theatre district stretched beyond Columbus Circle, leaving the Knickerbocker at the Southern-most boundary of the Broadway

LEFT : Interior demolition of Abbey's Theatre, 1930 (MCNY)

playhouses. Developers of the growing garment district had an eye on the theatre's 38th Street site. Hayman and company, unable to compete against over seventy newer playhouses in better locations, sold the theatre shortly after the stock market crash. Following a brief run of Philip

ABOVE : Abbey's Theatre interior, 1915 (TH)

Dunning's play *Sweet Land of Liberty* in 1930 the Knickerbocker was demolished.

ABOVE : Abbey's Theatre, at the northeast corner of Broadway and 38th Street. Renamed the Knickerbocker in 1896, this view dates from 1915. Next door is the Casino Theatre. (TH)

ABOVE : In 1895 Hammerstein's Olympia occupied the entire east side of Broadway between 44th and 45th streets. (NYHS)

OLYMPIA THEATRE

BROADWAY BETWEEN 44TH & 45TH STREETS   J.B. MCELFATRICK, 1895

Flush from his successes with the Manhattan and Harlem opera houses, Oscar Hammerstein moved into Long Acre Square, a neighborhood where the only theatre was the two-year old American. By January 1895 he had assembled several lots, including the charred remains of an old armory, for just over one million dollars. Ten months later the entire block on Broadway between 44th and 45th Streets was devoted to a shining new entertainment complex, the largest in the city. Oscar Hammerstein's press agents called it the most colossal amusement enterprise ever undertaken by a single manager. But to the thousands who flocked there opening night it was simply known as Hammerstein's Olympia. **T**he Olympia consisted of two main auditoriums, the Music Hall and Lyric, two smaller theatres, the Concert Hall and Roof Garden, plus an Oriental cafe, billiards, and bowling below street level. A single fifty-cent ticket allowed patrons to pass through two massive carved doorways into the marble foyer and sample all the entertainments in what could be considered the country's first multiplex theatre. **T**he 2,800-seat Olympia Music Hall, at the north end of the building, was the largest of the four theatres. Richly designed panels adorned the walls, ceiling, and proscenium, which was topped by a mural depicting Poetry and Prose being crowned by the goddess Fame. Decorated in the style of Louis XIV, the auditorium boasted 124 boxes in six proscenium tiers and five mezzanine tiers. It was the largest number of boxes in any existing place of amusement. In the center of the complex stood the Louis XV-style Concert Hall. Forty-three feet wide with a single balcony, the hall featured four twelve-foot tall female figures, each supporting a large crystal chandelier from its extended arms. Mirrors spanned the distance between the side wall pilasters and reflected the elaborate floral designs painted on the ceiling. South of the Concert Hall was the Lyric, a Louis XVI-style theatre with eighty-four boxes and room for about 1,700 persons. White and gold highlighted the auditorium of the Lyric, which, like the other halls, was rich with blue floral decorations. Spanning the three theatres was a glass-enclosed roof garden seating well over one thousand. Cooled by water cascading over the glass in summer and heated in winter, the Roof Garden offered entertainment all year long.

Even though the paint was still wet the Olympia opened as promised on 25 November 1895. (Opening before the paint was dry was something of a tradition at a Hammerstein theatre). The huge Music Hall boasted a vaudeville bill featuring one-legged clowns, aerialists, marionettes, quick change artists, and a female impersonator soprano. The Lyric, meanwhile, presented the most successful musical of the year, *Excelsior, Jr.* Other musicals followed at the Lyric, but unfortunately many of them were penned by Hammerstein himself. The failure of *Santa Maria* (which moved from the Music Hall) and *War Bubbles* added to the Olympia's growing debt and ultimately cost Hammerstein his theatres. On 29 June 1898, the Olympia was sold at auction by the New York Life Insurance Company. Hammerstein would recover, however, a few years later with the biggest success of his career, the Victoria. The Olympia, meanwhile, resurfaced as three separately operated theatres—The Music Hall, The Lyric, and The Roof Garden.

ABOVE : The Olympia Music Hall was known for its boxes—a record 124. (MCNY)

BELOW : The smaller Lyric Theatre was still one of the city's most elaborate playhouses. (MCNY)

The Music Hall became the New York Theatre when it reopened with Marie Dressler in *The Man in the Moon* in 1899. *Quo Vadis, Ben-Hur, Little Johnny Jones* (starring author George M. Cohan), *The Squaw Man,* and *Forty-five Minutes from Broadway* (also by Cohan) were among the productions that followed. Vaudeville played briefly in 1907, but legitimate drama returned the next year. Cohan was back in 1909 with the hit *The Man Who Owns Broadway,* and 1910 saw the smash *Naughty Marietta* on the New York's stage. In 1912 the name of the theatre was changed to the Moulin Rouge for Ziegfeld's production of *A Winsome Widow.* Leon Errol and Mae West were in the cast of this five-month hit. Errol stayed for the theatre's next show, *Ziegfeld Follies of 1912.* It ran for 11 weeks. In 1915, after a series of failures, the theatre was taken over by the Loew's circuit. For the next twenty years it presented films and vaudeville as Loew's New York.

The Lyric Theatre was leased to manager Charles Frohman, who rechristened it the Criterion for his 1899 production of Feydeau's *The Girl From Maxim's.* Appearances by Maude Adams in *The Little Minister* and Mrs. Leslie Carter in *Zaza* brought the playhouse into the twentieth century. 1904 saw separate performances by the Barrymore brothers at the Criterion—Lionel in *The Other Girl* and John in *The Dictator.* Many successes followed over the next few years, including *Miss Hook of Holland, The Bachelor's Baby,* and *Iphigenie en Aulide* danced by Isadora Duncan. The house showed movies as the Vitagraph starting in 1914 but was again known as the Criterion when the entertainment moved from the screen to the stage in 1916. Laurette Taylor and Lynn Fontanne made a hit out of *Happiness* in 1917, and the long-run record of 316 performances was set by John

ABOVE : The Olympia in 1929. (LAPL)

ABOVE : The Olympia Roof Garden as the Cherry Blossom Grove at the turn of the century. In 1907 Florenz Ziegfeld took over as manager of the Roof Garden and renamed it the Jardin de Paris. It was there that he produced the first five editions of his famous *Follies.* Later the space became a dance cabaret and finally, a movie theatre. (MCNY)

Golden's production of *Three Wise Fools* the following season. Lionel Barrymore returned in 1920 for the Criterion's final legitimate show, the drama *The Letter of the Law.* Following its 89 performances the screen went back in and movies took over for the next fifteen years. In 1935 the old Olympia was demolished, its debris joining the rubble of Hammerstein's Victoria in a landfill in New Jersey or Long Island. The smaller buildings that replaced it included a movie theatre called the Criterion. In 1989 that structure was rebuilt to include two legitimate theatres. Known as the Criterion Center, it has brought live drama back to that block of Broadway after more than fifty years.

ABOVE : Victoria Theatre, north west corner of Seventh Avenue and 42nd Street, in 1904. (MCNY)

VICTORIA THEATRE

SEVENTH AVENUE AT 42ND STREET J.B. McELFATRICK, 1899

In 1898 Oscar Hammerstein was bankrupt. His three-year effort with the Olympia had cost him over a million dollars, leaving him virtually penniless. An average man would have been humbled and discouraged by the experience, but not Hammerstein. Through a combination of genius, drive, and luck he was able to start construction of a new theatre within a few months of being wiped out. Gilley Moore's Market Stables, in the heart of Longacre Square at 42nd and Seventh, was the site Hammerstein chose for the theatre. Due to the entreprenuer's severe financial condition, it would be Broadway's only new playhouse built from second-hand materials. The stables' hayloft became part of the stage, rugs from a scrapped ocean liner covered the floor, and the seats came from one of the city's defunct theatres. Hammerstein even avoided hauling charges by dumping the construction debris in the hollow wall spaces and cut decorating costs by leaving the white plaster walls unpainted. When construction was completed after just nine months, Hammerstein christened his theatre the Victoria because, he explained, he had been victorious over his enemies. He had also won over the critics, judging by their response to the theatre on the 3 March 1899 opening night. "The Victoria, at a bird's eye view, looks like a big twinkling pearl," wrote the *New York American,* "all white and gold with the opals of electricity studding it in profusion . . . Gorgeous carpets, splendid lounges and all the ultra-elegance the metropolis loves were to be seen everywhere." *The New York Dramatic Mirror* was a bit more specific in its description of the playhouse:

> " The features which attract attention first are the wide, roomy promenades, which run all around the house at the rear of the orchestra boxes and balcony seats. Although the house seats only 1,200, there is room for 2,000 standees who have the privilege of sitting at small tables if they choose . . . The proscenium is square, the opening being 38 feet wide and 42 feet high. The decorations are in white and canary, with a little gold here and there. The effect is pretty, and the house has a very bright, cheery look, which is emphasized by the warm, red colors in the chairs, carpets, and hangings. "

The Victoria began life as a legitimate theatre with the Rogers Brothers in *A Reign of Error.* The Rogers, who were comedians in the style of Weber and Fields, appeared in three shows at the Victoria during its first eighteen months. Other early productions included *Miss Prinnt* starring Marie Dressler, the flop *Sweet Music* (purportedly written by Hammerstein himself under a pseudonym), Charles Dillingham's first musical *The Office Boy,* and *Lew Dockstader's Minstrel Show.* A total of eleven shows opened during the Victoria's first four years, but none of them was the smash hit that would have truly established the theatre. In 1904 Hammerstein and his son William changed the policy of the theatre to family variety, a combination of comedians, singers, and novelty acts, plus live appearances by notorious people in the news (i.e. acquitted murder suspects, bridge jumpers, etc.). Hammerstein's varieties developed into full-blown vaudeville which was without question the producer's most successful venture,

ABOVE : Paradise Roof Garden detail, with Oscar Hammerstein in inset, 1902. (TM)

generating enough profit to enable him to build the Manhattan Opera House on 34th Street. Audiences rushed to see W.C. Fields, the Keatons, Charlie Chaplin, Houdini, Bert Williams, the Four Cohans, the Seven Little Foys, Evelyn Nesbitt on her red velvet swing, and Flossie Crane, the belter from Coney Island who vanished from show business after eloping with a singing waiter (a job category of Hammerstein's own invention). Another big attraction of the Victoria was the theatre above it, the Paradise Roof Garden. The open-air showplace, which could be enclosed in foul weather, presented vaudeville during the hot summer months when the city's indoor theatres were closed. The Roof Garden spilled over to Hammerstein's adjacent Republic Theatre. There rooftop strollers could enjoy an actual Dutch-style dairy farm, complete with a live cow, chickens, ducks in a pond, a goat, and even a costumed milkmaid. (Seventy years later Eddie Foy, Jr. fondly remembered the warm, fresh glass of milk she gave him after he and his brothers finished their evening performance). To many New Yorkers, Broadway's barnyard was the best part of summer in the city.

The Victoria and the Paradise Roof Garden were eventually combined under one name—Hammerstein's. To have played Hammerstein's was every act's dream, and to have come "direct from Hammerstein's" ensured success on the road. For eleven years Oscar Hammerstein could be seen in the lobby of his theatre, wearing a silk top hat, puffing on a cigar, and more often than not eating a French pastry, keeping an eye on the acts that made his theatre the most famous amusement center in the world. By 1915 Hammerstein, who's true passion was grand opera, decided he had taken what he could out of his moneymaker and allowed a syndicate headed by S.L. "Roxy" Rothafel to take over the building. Much to Hammerstein's dismay they demolished the Seventh Avenue facade and gutted the interior, leaving only the three walls standing. Into this shell Roxy built Times Square's first movie palace, the Rialto, which opened in 1916. Nineteen years later the entire structure was razed and replaced with a four-story combination of shops and offices, plus a smaller movie theatre known as the Rialto.

BELOW : Paradise Roof Garden, 1902. A year earlier this theatre on top of the Victoria was enclosed and expanded to include a "Dutch dairy farm" above the adjacent Republic. (MCNY)

THEATRE REPUBLIC

207 WEST 42ND STREET ALBERT WESTOVER, 1900

After building six large theatres, some of them quite mammoth, Oscar Hammerstein eagerly described his latest project as the "perfect parlor theatre, compact in size, artistic in decoration, and complete in every detail . . . a drawing room of the drama, dedicated to all that is best in dramatic and lyric art." The Theatre Republic was immediately west of Hammerstein's Victoria, (which later annexed the Republic's roof as part of its own Paradise Roof Garden). The main feature of the handsome brownstone and brick theatre was its exterior marble double staircase leading to the second balcony which, with its own entrance and box office, was completely separate from the rest of the theatre. Just prior to the Republic's opening in 1900 *The New York Times* described how audiences would enter the theatre

" through three broad low doors, like Grecian gateways, into a lobby where are situated the box office, check room, information bureau, and cab office. From the lobby two gateways in similar style lead directly to the orchestra floor—which in this case is a misnomer since the orchestra, except during opera engagements, will be located in a gallery over the proscenium arch. On the left and right, respectively, as one enters are seen broad marble stairways with heavy carved and gilded balustrades leading to the first balcony or dress circle. There are only 1,100 large and comfortable loges, six proscenium boxes, plus a number of boxes set in the side walls of the theatre. The proscenium arch is thirty-five feet high from the stage level and is decorated with allegorical figures and classic designs in relief. Immediately above the arch the life-size figures representing Harmony and Melody, supporting between them a large golden lyre, mask the musician's balcony.

The decorations throughout the house are in harmony with those of the proscenium arch and boxes, the color scheme being green, ivory, and old gold. The commanding feature of the theatre is the great dome over the whole auditorium. This dome is gilded, and from it depends an immense chandelier, whose pale incandescents blend in marvelous effects with the upthrown cardinal lights concealed in the broad bottom rim of the dome. This forms an entirely novel scheme of interior decorations and illuminations, being a replica on a slightly smaller scale of the dome at the Capitol in Washington. "

Lionel Barrymore appeared in James A. Herne's play Sag Harbor on 27 September 1900 when the Theatre Republic openend. The first long run at the playhouse, however, began that New Year's Eve when In the Palace of the King started a six-month residency. In September 1902, Hammerstein gave producer David Belasco a long-term lease on the Republic, which Belasco renamed after himself. Belasco also made some exterior alterations to the theatre. Decorative metalwork enclosed the staircases, an elaborate glass canopy covered the main entrance, and a medallion naming the structure "Hammerstein's Theatre Republic" was removed. Belasco's remodeling of the Republic's interior was extensive. The balcony fronts were simplified and

the musician's gallery, proscenium mosaics, and luxurious wall brocades were replaced by more subdued decorations in autumn brown and green. In contrast to these somber tones, the boxes were draped in rich rose silk damask. Backstage, Belasco made his theatre the best equipped in the city by adding traps, elevator lifts, and turntables. While digging out an extra twenty feet below the stage to accomodate these new devices, the excavation crew hit an underground spring that flooded the house, causing an additional $125,000 damage.

LEFT : The Republic under construction in 1900. (MCNY)
BELOW : The original lobby, 1900. (MCNY)

ABOVE : The original auditorium in 1900. (MCNY)

For eight years Belasco produced a string of hits featuring present and future stars, including David Warfield, Jane Cowl, George Arliss, Mrs. Leslie Carter, and Tyrone Power. The last production of 1907 was also memorable for its cast. *The Warrens of Virginia* showcased the acting talents of Cecil B. de Mille and Mary Pickford. In 1910 Belasco returned the house to its original name when he decided to retitle the Stuyvesant, (a theatre he had built three years earlier), after himself. That theatre is still called the Belasco.

Mary Pickford returned to the Republic in 1913's *A Good Little Devil,* co-starring Lillian Gish, and Jane Cowl came back for *Common Clay,* a 316-performance hit in 1915. *Lilac Time, Parlor, Bedroom, and Bath,* and *The Sign on the Door* were a few of the more successful shows that followed in the next seven years, but none could match the runaway hit that was to occupy the Republic for six seasons. After a faltering start at the Fulton Theatre in 1922, *Abie's Irish Rose* transferred to the Republic. With the help of cut-rate tickets sold by Joe Leblang in Gray's Drugstore, the Irish-Jewish comedy built into a record-breaking success. When it finally closed in 1928, *Abie's Irish Rose* had played 2,327 times, a record for the day and still one of Broadway's longest runs.

Many shows have their good-luck charms, and *Abie's Irish Rose* was no exception. In 1929 the story of the show's lucky horseshoe was reported by *The New York Herald Tribune.* "It was nailed over the stage door soon after the play started its record-breaking run, and it was taken down the night the play closed. When *My Girl Friday* went into the Republic Theatre, according to the Associated Press, a stagehand, browsing

ABOVE : 42nd Street in 1924. (TH)

OPPOSITE PAGE :
TOP : A 1903 view, one year after David Belasco renamed the house. (NYHS)
BOTTOM : Interior following Belasco's renovations. (MCNY)

around dusty corners, found the horseshoe. The doormen polished it, found a stepladder, and nailed it securely above their post of duty. That night the show was raided."

A few more shows carried the Republic into the thirties, but the character of 42nd Street was changing. Movies were more popular than ever, and many theatre managers had discovered that they were able to make more money charging ten cents a seat six times a day than they could waiting around for the rare legitimate hit. In February 1931 the Republic stopped waiting for lightning to hit twice and converted to modern burlesque from Billy Minsky, the most famous purveyor of the strip-tease. He kept the

49

ABOVE : Billy Minsky's burlesque was one of 1933's most popular entertainments. (TH)

BELOW : Before its rebirth as a children's theatre, the Republic played X-rated films. (NvH)

bumps grinding until 1942. In a burst of wartime patriotism, the name of the theatre was changed to the Victory when it began showing second-run movies that same year. Pornographic films attracted a new clientele in the seventies and eighties, but mainstream films were on the bill when the theatre closed for restoration in the early nineties. Before the work began, however, the Victory presented *Crowbar*, a site-specific play about the construction of the theatre. It was the first live drama on Forty-second Street since the tabloid plays at the Selwyn in 1950. A key part of the plan to revitalize Forty-second Street was an $18 million fund created by the developers of four large office towers. The city and state earmarked the money for the restoration of two historic theatres to be used as non-profit houses. The Victory was the first to benefit from the fund, with $11.4 million spent restoring the theatre to its appearance during Belasco's heyday and adapting it for use as the city's first full-time theatre for children and families.

The New Victory opened in December 1995 to glowing reviews for both the renovation and the theatre's programs. In the first year ninety-three thousand people attended the shows at the New Victory. It is only fitting that Times Square's oldest existing theatre, with a past so strongly linked to the men who made Broadway great, should be the first of Broadway's lost theatres to be found.

OPPOSITE, ABOVE LEFT : Auditorium, 1989. (MH)

OPPOSITE, ABOVE RIGHT : Cherubim perch on the rim of the auditorium dome in 1997. The interior of the Victory was restored to Belasco's period. (AM)

OPPOSITE, BELOW : The rebuilt exterior staircase and standing lamps recall Hammerstein's era. The New Victory signs are modern. (NvH)

ABOVE : Circle interior, 1905. (MCNY)

CIRCLE THEATRE

1825 BROADWAY AT 60TH STREET CHARLES CAVENAUGH, 1901 · THOMAS W. LAMB, 1906

At the turn of the century it was clear that 42nd Street would soon become the center for legitimate theatre in New York. While all eyes were on Oscar Hammerstein and his efforts with the Victoria and Republic, two enterprising owners of a long-forgotten music hall were struggling to open Columbus Circle's first place of entertainment.

Charles Evans and W.D. Mann looked to the growing population of the Upper West Side to support the Circle Music Hall, which would attract audiences with weekly bills of high-class, polite vaudeville suitable for entire families. Although the area's residents looked forward to having their own theatre by the fall of 1900, one of the music hall's neighbors effectively closed the house before it even opened. One block east of the Circle stood the church of The Paulist Fathers, a group that frowned upon light entertainments such as vaudeville. When the elders learned what Evans and Mann had in mind, they exercised their rights as a religious organization to maintain a theatre-free zone around their church. With the music hall nearing completion, the two builders nevertheless filed their application for an operating license. After the strenuous objections of the Paulist Fathers, the license was denied. The battle to open was a bitter one, lasting well into the following year. Finally the church relented when it was promised that the theatre would only present high-class orchestra concerts. This may have pleased the Fathers, but it left the working-class neighbors generally unamused. After briefly opening in 1901, the Circle closed deeply in the red. A further accord was ultimately reached with the church. When the music hall reopened under new management in 1902, it was as a legitimate theatre. With deep red walls accented by olive green and old gold designs, the theatre was ornate and attractive. The orchestra floor was heavily carpeted and surrounded by boxes. A second tier of boxes took the place of a standard balcony, and the good-sized stage was framed by a square proscenium. Sitting in separate cane-bottom chairs, patrons were allowed to smoke and drink while watching a performance. The Circle Theatre's legitimate career began with the Herbert Stock Company's production of the play *Aristocracy*. A policy of popular-priced vaudeville followed, but when the nearby Colonial Theatre opened in 1905 with vaudeville of its own the Circle switched to burlesque. Early motion pictures also became one of the amusements at the Circle. In 1906 architect Thomas Lamb was hired to thoroughly remodel the theatre. He increased the height of the auditorium, added a second balcony, and redesigned the Broadway entrance in preparation for the shows that were booked into the uptown house. In 1908 the first of four successive musicals played the Circle. Composer Gus Edwards' *The Merry-Go-Round* was enough of a hit to warrant renaming the house Gus Edwards' Music Hall during its run. His next show, *School Days,* was a four-week flop. *The Queen of the*

ABOVE : Circle Theatre, 1905. (MCNY)

Moulin Rouge followed, and kept the theatre open for five months. The Circle's final legitimate show, a blackface musical called *In Hayti,* squeaked out a seven-week run in the fall of 1909. The Circle returned to the more familiar territory of vaudeville, burlesque, and movies for the next twenty-nine years. For twenty-one of those years the house was part of the Loews chain, but that group gave it up during the depression. As an independently operated movie house, the Circle fell victim to the theatre labor disputes of 1935 when a bomb seriously damaged the box office and lobby. A month later the theatre was sold at auction. In 1939 the interior of the Circle was demolished and rebuilt as the Columbus Circle Roller Rink, but the exterior remained until the site was cleared for the construction of the New York Convention Center in 1954.

ABOVE : Circle Theatre, 1908. Lessee Lawrence Mulligan is pictured in the upper corner. (LC)

BELOW : Columbus Circle, 1908. This westerly view includes the Majestic and Circle theatres. (NYHS)

MAJESTIC THEATRE

5 COLUMBUS CIRCLE   JOHN H. DUNCAN, 1903

Today New York's Columbus Circle is a confusing, oval-shaped jumble of streets choked with bumper-to-bumper traffic and shoulder-to-shoulder pedestrians. At the start of the twentieth century, though, the place where Broadway meets Eighth Avenue was an elegant round plaza at the southwest corner of Central Park known as Grand Circle. As the theatre district gradually expanded into Times Square, a few enterprising developers speculated that the next major center for entertainment would actually be established twenty blocks to the north. E.D. Stair and A.L. Wilbur were counting on just that to happen when they began construction of their new Majestic Theatre in 1902.

Designed by John H. Duncan, the Majestic presented a narrow profile to the Circle while the auditorium itself extended west, fronting both 58th and 59th Streets. Mounted below a round paned-glass window, two carved stone theatre masks watched over patrons as they entered the Majestic through its circular lobby. In a wide promenade behind the orchestra seats a double staircase climbed to the theatre's two balconies, which swept towards the stage at a modest rake. The configuration of the balcony seats was unique, with rear aisles omitted in favor of cross-over aisles placed midway on each tier. Frequently employed in Europe, it was the first time this arrangement was used in New York. None of the 1,354 seats was blocked by pillars, thanks to the relatively new cantilever system of supporting the balconies on immense steel beams. **T**he auditorium was decorated in green and gold, with white relief around the stage apron, proscenium, exits, and in the four trumpeting statues above the boxes. Watered silk panels covered the walls above white marble wainscoting. Behind the velour curtain, with its gold fringe and braid, was a stage thirty-six feet deep and eighty-feet wide, adequate to handle the requirements of any show. **T**he Majestic opened on 20 January with the biggest hit of the 1903 season. The first musical version of *The Wizard of Oz,* starring Fred Stone and Dave Montgomery as the Scarecrow and Tin Man, was acclaimed for its elaborate scenic effects, particularly the opening cyclone. Victor Herbert's *Babes in Toyland* lit up the Majestic following Oz's ten-month run and managed to enthrall uptown theatregoers through April 1904. *The Top of the World, Bandanna Land,* and *The Quaker Girl* were other early hits at the theatre, the latter reopening the house as the Park in 1911. Musicals and plays, along with Sunday movie shows, continued to attract audiences during the next ten years. In 1914 Mrs. Patrick Campbell starred there in the U.S. premiere of Shaw's *Pygmalion,* and in later seasons Helen Hayes, Edward G. Robinson, George Arliss, and the Society of American Singers appeared at the Park. **A**lthough legitimate attractions had kept the theatre in business for almost twenty years, the Park's managers opted to switch to the more reliable policy of burlesque in 1922, changing the name to Minsky's Park Music Hall in the process. A year later William Randolph Hearst took over the playhouse as a prime outlet for his Cosmopolitan Pictures. He changed the name again; this time, not surprisingly, to the Cosmopolitan. In 1925 Florenz Ziegfeld took over the house, refurbished it with the

LEFT : Green, ivory, and gold were the majestic's predominant colors in 1903. (MCNY)

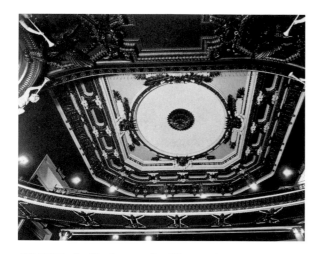

ABOVE : Auditorium and ceiling, 1903. (MCNY)

BELOW : The Majestic brought musical comedy to the Grand Circle in 1903. (MCNY)

help of his chief designer Joseph Urban, and brought musical comedy back to its stage in the form of Sigmund Romberg's *Louie the 14th,* starring Leon Errol and Ethel Shutta. It was a nine-month hit. After Ziegfeld left to concentrate on building his own theatre in 1926, the Cosmopolitan suffered from the competition of the newer, more conveniently located playhouses. Successful bookings were harder to come by, and even the sure things didn't pay off. Vincent Youmans' *Hit the Deck* had been a huge hit, and everyone agreed his 1929 show at the Cosmopolitan, *Great Day,* had a great score. But not even the title number, "More Than You Know," and "Without A Song" could make audiences forget the stock

ABOVE : As William Randolph Hearst's Cosmopolitan movie theatre in 1924. (TH)

market crash. The show closed after only 36 performances. In 1931 the theatre reverted to showing films and vaudeville (called "Cosmo Varieties") and was booked occasionally as a rehearsal hall. It briefly returned to the legitimate in 1934 as The Theatre of Young America, but in 1935 reverted to showing movies as the Park. Nine years passed before the theatre's next legitimate booking. Renamed the International in October 1944, its dressing rooms were once again occupied, this time by members of the *Ballet International*. Alfred Drake, Burl Ives, and the cast of *Sing Out, Sweet Land* followed in December. The last month of 1945 saw another name change, to the Columbus Circle, but "International" was back up on the marquee by the following August. The bookings that followed were singularly unsuccessful and in 1948 the International's owner, Marquis George De Cuevas, offered to loan the theatre to City Center. The offer was declined. The Marquis then restored the house, hoping the booking jam might push a few shows his way. The International was considered much too far out of the mainstream, though, and the house stood empty while even such fringe theatres as the Century played hits. In 1949 the theatre at last had a tenant—the NBC television network. As one of its first theatre-studios, many of the network's early programs originated from the International, including Sid Caesar's classic *Your Show of Shows*. When the network's lease expired in 1954 there was little question as to what would happen to the International. It was demolished in June of that year to provide wider pedestrian access to the city's new convention center.

LYRIC THEATRE

213 WEST 42ND STREET   V. HUGO KOEHLER, 1903

Reginald DeKoven's enormously popular (and profitable) 1890 musical *Robin Hood* had been touring the country for 13 years when the author decided to use part of his windfall to build a theatre devoted to the type of light opera that made him so wealthy. The Shubert brothers agreed to sell DeKoven a site they owned on 42nd Street in return for a twenty-one year lease to run the new building, giving them not only another Broadway playhouse but also a brand new suite of offices from which to run their operation.

The exterior of the Lyric Theatre was beautiful. Lyres, theatre masks, and reclining muses decorated the facade of the narrow entrance tucked between the Republic and Times Square theatres on 42nd Street. Above the lobby, behind a huge arched window, was the office space occupied by the Shuberts. The light apple green and rose-colored auditorium, on the 43rd Street end of the T-shaped plot, was broad and shallow in an effort to bring the 1,261 seats as close as possible to the stage. Old ivory and gold plaster reliefs decorated the ceiling and gave a sense of luxury to even those seated in the gallery, while the well-heeled patron had a choice of 18 boxes from which to see and be seen. By far, however, the most impressive aspect of the building's design was its 43rd Street facade. If the Lyric name, or the words "drama" and "music" had not been carved in the white stone, a passerby could easily have mistaken the theatre for a grand private mansion in the Italian Renaissance style. The brick and terra-cotta, copper roof and iron balconies, and three stories of exquisitely carved windows created a rich, stately appearance not common to Broadway theatres. But instead of bringing guests into the reception hall of a manor house, the doors under the iron and glass canopy opened to the auditorium, stage, and stairway leading to the labyrinth of fourth floor rehearsal halls where many Shubert shows took shape. The flamboyant star Richard Mansfield, who was under the Shuberts' management, opened the Lyric in *Old Heidelburg* on 12 October 1903. Two years later Douglas Fairbanks was featured in the smash production of *Fantana*. This 1905 musical was the last to bear the credit "Sam S. Shubert offers"; the young producer was killed in a train accident during *Fantana*'s six-month run. His brothers and partners Lee and J.J. continued to run the theatre empire that grew to dominate Broadway. An operetta based on Shaw's *Arms and the Man, The Chocolate Soldier,* began an impressive 296-performance run in 1909, followed in 1911 by the American premiere of Ibsen's *The Lady and the Sea.* Two major contributors to the theatre made their Broadway debuts in 1912's *The Firefly*—composer Rudolf Friml and producer Arthur Hammerstein. Friml continued his success at the Lyric with *High Jinks* the following season. A number of successful plays and musicals, plus the occasional movie, carried the Lyric into the twenties, the decade in which the theatre had its most memorable productions. Fred and Adele Astaire appeared before a cheering Broadway audience in 1922's *For Goodness Sake.* In 1925 Irving Berlin and George S. Kaufman provided the framework for the Marx Brothers' crazy antics in their second hit, *The Cocoanuts.* Comedians Bobby Clark and Paul McCullough propelled *The Ramblers* to 289

LEFT : The 42nd Street entrance to the Lyric Theatre in 1903. (MCNY)

ABOVE : Nearing completion in 1903. (MCNY)

showings in 1926, just as Florenz Ziegfeld guided his production of Friml's *The Three Musketeers* to a seven-month stay in 1928. It proved to be the composer's final successful show. The next season Cole Porter claimed his rightful place beside the hitmakers with his thirty-week smash *Fifty Million Frenchmen.* Porter's show was the last long-run to play the Lyric. A marionette musical in 1932 and the black drama *Run Little Chillun'* in 1933 each ran fifteen weeks but neither generated enough income to keep the depression's creditors from the door. After the three-week flop of *Gypsy Blonde* in 1934 the Lyric joined its neighbors on 42nd Street and switched to movies. Over the years the boxes were removed and the 43rd Street marquee was dismantled as the elaborate facade darkened under the city's grime and soot.

In 1996 the Canadian theatrical firm Livent signed a long-term lease for the Lyric and adjacent Apollo. After meticulously removing hundreds of decorative plaster elements from both buildings, the theatre auditoriums and stages were razed. Only the 43rd Street Italian Renaissance facade of the Lyric, the 42nd Street lobby of the Apollo, and the 42nd Street exteriors of both houses were left standing. Rising out of the rubble on 43rd Street is a new 1,839-seat theatre, designed to be the district's second-largest. The salvaged architectural elements, restored to their original condition, are to be incorporated into the new auditorium and lobbies. The Ford Center for the Performing Arts links past to present by combining the best parts of the old theatres into a modern stage facility sponsored by the Detroit automaker. The $30 million playhouse, the first free-standing legitimate theatre to be built in Times Square in seventy years, is scheduled to open in January 1998 with the musical *Ragtime*.

Drawings of the Ford Center for the Performing Arts, which incorporates both the Lyric and Apollo theatres, appear in the Appendix on page 257.

ABOVE : The Lyric's finished interior, 1903. (MCNY)

ABOVE : The Lyric's ornate 43rd Street entrance during the 1903 run of the its second show, *The Red Feather*. (DPL)

ABOVE : Lyric auditorium, 1989. (MH)

LEFT : The 42nd Street exterior in 1989. (MH)

BELOW : Detail of the 43rd Street facade, 1989. (MH)

HUDSON THEATRE

141 WEST 44TH STREET   J.B. MCELFATRICK, ISRAELS & HARDER, 1903

With the opening of the Hudson on 19 October 1903 the boundaries of the theatre district continued to grow. Producer Henry B. Harris' playhouse had entrances on both 44th and 45th streets (for patrons and performers, respectively) and was the first theatre to open on either avenue. The premiere production, *Cousin Kate* starring Ethel Barrymore, lasted only six weeks. The new theatre, on the other hand, began a very long run.

The four-story Renaissance-style facade of the Hudson's main entrance complemented the modest brownstones that neighbored the theatre, and gave few clues to the riches to be found inside the playhouse. Past the front doors, audiences discovered a dazzling combination of Greco-Roman motifs, indirect lighting, and Tiffany glass. From the marble box-office guarded by four bronze heads of Hermes, the Greek god of commerce and eloquence, massive brass and bronze doors opened to the largest foyer of any theatre at that time. The hundred-foot long lobby was colored in soft tones of green, orange, and old ivory. It featured six archways subdivided by salon-glass mirrors, low relief friezes suggested by similar works of art in the Roman Baths of Titus, and a triple-domed ceiling of Tiffany glass. The auditorium had seating for nearly 1,100 in its orchestra and two balconies. Like the foyer, the proscenium arch also had Roman friezes, only this time they were copied from the House of Nero. Bay leaf bands and mosaic panels studded with iridescent glass added to its unconventional look. The silk velour house curtain of green and yellow matched the muted upholstery in the rest of the theatre, which was warmly illuminated by concealed lighting surrounding the stage and direct lighting from small fixtures imbedded in the plaster latticework of the ceiling. The only vivid colors in the auditorium came from Tiffany glass mosaics in the fronts of the balconies and upper boxes. Critical response to the Hudson, as it was to most of the city's new playhouses, was quite positive. But although the comfortable and dignified decor of the theatre was admired, at least one critic felt that the overall effect lacked character. "One wishes for a few notes of virility," wrote *Architectural Record,* "and for some big, strong masses of color somewhere in the ensemble. The theatre is pretty, but it is very tame." Nine years after the Hudson opened, Harris and his wife returned from a trip to Europe aboard the brand-new liner *RMS Titanic.* The ship struck an iceberg midway through its maiden voyage and went down in the freezing waters of the North Atlantic. Harris was one of the 1,500 passengers and crew who lost his life in the disaster. His wife Rene was the last person to leave the ship in a lifeboat, however, and took over the management of the theatre shortly after her rescue.

The Hudson enjoyed many successes in the following years, and was considered one of New York's top theatres. In 1929 Mrs. Harris turned down an offer to sell the Hudson for over $1,000,000. But within three years, thanks to the crash and depression, Mrs. Harris joined the ranks of insolvent theatrical producers. Her beloved theatre was sold in foreclosure to the Emigrant Industrial Savings Bank for only $100,000.

CBS bought the theatre in 1934 and converted it for use as a radio studio. A glass-enclosed control booth added for the network broadcasts was removed in 1937 when the house returned to legitimate theatre. In 1943 a syndicate led by playwrights Howard Lindsay and Russell Crouse purchased the Hudson. (Lindsay

ABOVE : Hudson Theatre interior prior to the 1903 opening. (MCNY)

claimed the theatre was actually named for his father, Hudson Highland Lindsay, who was born on a ship as it passed through the Hudson River highlands.) The theatre stayed open with a series of plays including *Arsenic and Old Lace* (moved over from the Fulton Theatre), *Detective Story*, and Lindsay and Crouse's own Pulitzer Prize-winning comedy, *State of the Union*.

The syndicate sold the Hudson to NBC for $595,000 in 1950. For the next decade the theatre was in constant use as a television studio for such live programs as *Broadway Open House, Feather Your Nest,* and *The Tonight Show*. In 1959, after many shows had moved to Los Angeles, NBC turned off the cameras and spent $100,000 restoring the Hudson to its former glory. It was during this period that the odd story of Robert Breen came to light. **S**ince 1942 Mr. Breen, a theatrical producer, had been living in the Hudson Theatre with his wife and family. Renting nine rooms on the third and fourth floors, he made his own repairs and took care of his own janitorial needs. Heat and hot water were available to him only when the theatre was in use; during dark periods (sometimes months at a stretch) he relied on electric heaters and fireplaces. Needing his "apartment" for of-

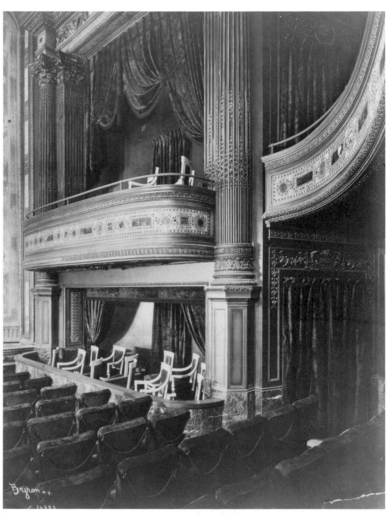

ABOVE : The Hudson's boxes, 1903. (MCNY)

fice space, NBC asked Mr. Breen to move. He refused, forcing the network to seek a court order of dispossession. This tactic failed, and finally NBC had to lease the theatre with the Breens as part of the package. In 1990 members of the Breen family still live in the Hudson Theatre. **T**he Hudson returned to legitimate theatre with *Davy Jones' Locker,* a marionette musical that sank without a trace after a brief run. Lillian Hellman's *Toys in the Attic* was more successful, managing to keep the theatre in business for over a year. In 1961 a Manhattan garage operator revealed plans to buy the Hudson, demolish it, and use the site as a parking lot. This announcement was not well-received by the press. To its credit NBC decided to back out of the sale. The network's lease on their primary east coast color studio, the Ziegfeld Theatre, had expired and the Hudson was intended for use as its replacement. This never came about, however, and the following year NBC had a change of heart and put the Hudson up for sale. For the next twenty-five years the Hudson would change owners and policies with alarming frequency, each time barely avoiding the wrecker's ball.

After a short-lived production of *Strange Interlude* in 1963, the Hudson went dark for two years. The lights went on in 1965 for *This Was Burlesque,* Ann Corio's successful revue featuring bad comics and buxom strippers. Following *Burlesque,* the playhouse again became the target of developers. This time the plan was to gut the interior and con-

ABOVE : The marble and brass box-office, 1990. (NvH)

vert it into a multi-level parking structure. But fortunately the builders were denied a permit by the city, and soon the Hudson changed hands for the fourth time in four years. The new owner acquired it as part of the site for an office development, but abandoned the idea as demand for office space waned. Following a three-week return to legit with *How To Be A Jewish Mother* in late 1967, the Hudson was leased by the Avon chain of pornographic movie theatres. For seven years the playhouse that had been home to Barrymore, Cohan, and Fiske, presented 16mm entertainments with titles like *Blow Below the Belt* and *Boys in the Attic*. In 1975 porno was ousted. The theatre was cleaned up and reopened showing second-run double features for a dollar, but the policy flopped and the Hudson closed. Concert promoter Ron Delsener gave the Hudson a new coat of paint and a new name, the Savoy, when he opened it as a rock venue and nightclub in 1980. It didn't catch on with the "in-crowd," however, and by 1983 rock was out. In the mid-eighties, anyone looking to buy a luxury condominium could have found a full-scale model of one such apartment constructed on the Hudson's stage. When the developer sold out the condo, the theatre closed. But thanks to the Landmarks Preservation Commission, all was not lost for the Hudson. In 1987 landmark status was granted for both the interior and exterior of the theatre, effectively protecting it from the next round of parking lot wars. Soon afterward developer Harry Macklowe constructed a large hotel adjacent to the Hudson and, unable to raze the theatre, incorporated it into the new building as a multipurpose auditorium and conference center. Although the Hudson may never again house a legitimate production, this grand old theatre still welcomes audiences for business meetings, lectures, fashion shows, and similar special events.

TOP: In 1974 the Hudson was a porno house. (NvH)

BOTTOM : View of the Hudson interior in 1990, with the theatre in use as a marketing center for the adjacent hotel. (NvH)

NEW AMSTERDAM THEATRE

214 WEST 42ND STREET   HERTS & TALLANT, 1903

Architects of the theatres constructed along Broadway at the turn of the century owed a considerable debt to builders of the past. The Moorish, Venetian, and Renaissance styles of their playhouses appealed to popular tastes while ignoring new ideas in design and art. In fact, only two of Broadway's ninety theatres reflected creative styles of the period in which they were built. George Keister's Earl Carroll Theatre was a dazzling 1931 Art Deco showplace while Herts and Tallant's 1903 masterpiece, the New Amsterdam Theatre, brought Art Nouveau to Broadway with spectacular success. Touted as the first complete use of Art Nouveau throughout an entire building, the New Amsterdam stood out among the shops, brownstones, churches, and other theatres of 42nd Street. The elaborate stone carvings, floral scrolls, and curved windows of the facade were crowned by five figures perched on a broad arch: a knight, his maiden, and three statues meant to represent comedy, music, and drama. Friezes depicting scenes from Shakespeare, Wagner, and Faust decorated the lobby while bas reliefs contrasting the old and new cities of New Amsterdam adorned the foyer, carved into the walls beneath the colored-glass dome that formed the ceiling. Vines and flowers were the primary motifs of the lobbies as well as the auditorium and promenade behind it, where animal heads were modeled into the emerald-green porcelain that covered the marble balustrades of the staircase. Allegorical murals decorated the walls above the elaborate proscenium and boxes. The largest of these panels, 45 feet x 18 feet, presented the victory of Art and Truth over Falsehood. Rich wood wainscoting lined the each side of the house, which was colored in tones of green, mother of pearl, and mauve. The orchestra, two balconies, and twelve boxes could seat an audience of 1,750. An elaborate Irish marble fireplace in the lounge and a richly-painted ceiling dome above the Art Nouveau archways of the smoking room made these spaces as luxurious as the rest of the building. An overwhelming success, the critical response to the showplace was summed up by *The New York Dramatic Mirror:* "The New Amsterdam Theatre is beyond question the most gorgeous playhouse in New York. Architecturally it is near perfection." Since a scene from the play decorated the lobby, it was only appropriate that the New Amsterdam open with *A Midsummer Night's Dream.* The Klaw and Erlanger production, starring Nat Goodwin, began its critically acclaimed run on 26 October 1903. New Amsterdam audiences enjoyed performances by Maxine Elliott, Richard Mansfield, James O'Neill (father of the future playwright), and William S. Hart during the playhouse's first decade and helped the musicals *Madame Sherry, The Pink Lady,* and *The Merry Widow* achieve record-breaking runs. (The success of 1907's *The Merry Widow* was phenomenal; it influenced everything from ladies' fashions to popular dancing and made operettas the rage of Broadway.)

LEFT : New Amsterdam Theatre, 1903. (NYHS)

NEW AMSTERDAM THEATRE

ABOVE : New Amsterdam Theatre, 1907. (NYHS)

In 1913 Florenz Ziegfeld began his long affiliation with the New Amsterdam. The first six editions of his *Follies* were runaway hits at the Jardin de Paris (the old New York Roof Garden). With *Follies of 1913* he moved the theatre's most popular revue to what had become Broadway's most popular musical house. Ziegfeld opened twelve separate *Follies* at the New Amsterdam, each more spectacular than the one before it. He filled the stage with talent. Headliners W.C. Fields, Ed Wynn, Bert Williams, Will Rogers, Fanny Brice, and Eddie Cantor attracted enough of a crowd to pack the roof theatre for *The Midnight Frolics*

ABOVE : New Amsterdam Theatre interior, 1903. (MCNY)

after each *Follies* performance. Although the *Follies* occasionally played other houses (including the Ziegfeld in 1931), the elaborate musicals would forever be associated with the New Amsterdam. The theatre's biggest hit came in 1920. It was produced by Ziegfeld but surprisingly was not one of his *Follies. Sally,* a book musical scored by Jerome Kern and Victor Herbert, starred Marilyn Miller and Leon Errol and lasted a remarkable 570 performances. Five years later *Sunny,* also with Miller and by Kern, came in second in the long-run derby with 517 showings. In 1928 George Gershwin and Sigmund Romberg collaborated on the score of *Rosalie,* a ten month hit. It was followed by Eddie Cantor in *Whoopee,* and *Earl Carroll's Vanities of 1930*. Fred and Adele Astaire lit up *The Band Wagon* in 1931 and Moss Hart and Irving Berlin brought forth *Face the Music* the next season. When *Revenge with Music* opened in 1934 the New Amsterdam was the only venue still devoted to legitimate theatre on 42nd Street. Yet despite competition from the boulevard's movie and burlesque houses, *Revenge with Music* enjoyed a profitable run. *George White's Scandals*

of 1936 couldn't make the same claim, although Bert Lahr, Willie and Eugene Howard, and Rudy Vallee did their best to bring the New Amsterdam back to the glory days of the big-time revue. The Romberg operetta *Forbidden Melody* tried to take the audience even further back, but it too was unsuccessful. The circle was completed when *Othello* was staged at the New Amsterdam in January 1937. Just as *A Midsummer*

LEFT : Smoking lounge, 1903. (MCNY)

ABOVE : New Amsterdam Theatre, 1925. (WISC)

BELOW : Lobby, 1925. Elevators to the roof garden each held 50 persons. (WISC)

Night's Dream had started the magnificent theatre's life as a legitimate playhouse, so did *Othello* end it. After its three-week run the movie screen went up and live theatre left 42nd Street. Conversion to a movie theatre brought some changes to the New Amsterdam. The figures and decorations of the 42nd Street facade were chiseled off and the arch was reduced to a plain white curve. As was the case with most former legitimate houses, the boxes (along with the plaster flora above them) were removed to provide better sight lines for the screen. For forty-six years the New Amsterdam stood, slightly scarred but still the street's most beautiful theatre. Only the occasional appearance of the ghost of *Follies* showgirl Olive Thomas (seen standing on the stage by the theatre's handyman) provided a haunting reminder of the New Amsterdam's glamorous past.

By 1982 the New Amsterdam had been designated a New York City landmark and was placed on the National Register of Historic Places. That same year the Nederlander Organization, the second largest operator of legit houses in the city, gained control of the theatre. In 1983 the building went dark as millions were spent on its restoration. The work was halted, however, when major steel beams were found to be corroded. Holes in the roof and windows allowed rain and snow to enter the building for the five years that followed, causing extensive cosmetic and structural damage. When the state purchased the New Amsterdam for $247,000 in 1992 its condition was deplorable. It looked as if restoration would only be possible by a tenant with deep pockets and a lot of clout. In 1993 just such a tenant materialized. **T**he Walt Disney Company wanted to establish a permanent presence on Broadway; the New Amsterdam provided the perfect opportunity. But Disney's willingness to take on the challenge of the decaying landmark did not come without a price. The company held out for low-interest government loans to subsidize $26 million of the estimated $34 million cost of the restoration. Disney also insisted that at least two other major entertainment companies would have to lease properties on the street before it would go forward. When Madame Tussaud's and AMC

BELOW : Foyer, 1925. (WISC)

signed up for the Harris and Empire, respectively, Disney committed.

After two years of intensive work, a showplace lost to live theatre for over sixty years has been restored to its turn-of-the-century splendor. The New Amsterdam's exquisite murals and whimsical relief carvings constantly surprise and amuse, taking visitors back to a long-gone era when the theatre building itself was part of the attraction. Steeped in the history of Broadway, the New Amsterdam has survived time and the elements to emerge as one of the district's most beautiful playhouses.

RIGHT : Coat check, 1925. (WISC)

BELOW : Box Office, 1925. Tickets were sold for both the main auditorium and the Frolic Theatre on the roof. (WISC)

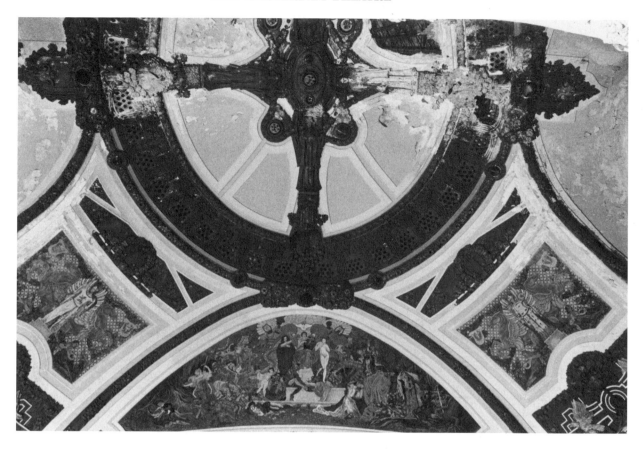

ABOVE : The damaged ceiling, 1990. (MH)

RIGHT : New Amsterdam auditorium, 1990. (MH)

RIGHT : The theatre's unrestored foyer in 1990. (MH)

BELOW LEFT : The grand reopening of the New Amsterdam took place in May 1997 with a concert staging of the new musical *King David*. A fully-staged version of the animated hit *The Lion King* was scheduled to follow. The theatre's landmarked art deco marquee, installed in 1947, was refurbished during the theatre's total restoration. (WC)

BELOW RIGHT : The newly reconstructed boxes of the New Amsterdam in 1997. (WC)

TOP : On the roof of the New Amsterdam was a fully-equipped, 680-seat theatre called the Aerial Gardens. Painted in shades of old rose and green, and decorated with murals, the theatre presented legitimate shows each summer beginning in 1904. But in 1910, when the main theatre downstairs became air-cooled, (allowing it to stay open year-round), the Aerial Gardens closed. Florenz Ziegfeld reopened it in 1915 as the Danse de Follies, presenting his late-night Midnight Frolic there until 1921. Two years later it reopened with legit offerings as the Dresden, but was soon renamed the Frolic in an attempt to recapture its earlier popularity. It couldn't compete with other houses in the area, however, and in 1930 became a radio studio. Twenty years later television followed, and in the succeeding decades it was also used as a rehearsal hall. This photograph dates from 1925. (TH)

CENTER : An attempt to return the New Amsterdam Roof to legitimate use in 1983 failed when serious structural flaws were discovered. Although the lobby, stage, and dressing rooms remain intact, the auditorium was gutted. (MH)

BOTTOM : The balcony stairs, along with a small mural and some broken plasterwork, was all that remained of the theatre's auditorium in 1990. (MH)

LIBERTY THEATRE

234 WEST 42ND STREET   HERTS & TALLANT, 1904

In an age when most playhouses were decorated in exotic foreign styles, whether they be Moorish, rococo, or Renaissance, the patriotic motifs of Klaw and Erlanger's Liberty Theatre must have been a welcome sight to students of theatre design. The theatre itself was on 41st Street, but in 1904 there was little attraction to opening in that location, especially when four popular theatres had their main entrances just one block north. The 100-foot lobby that architects Herts & Tallent created did provide the Liberty with a 42nd Street entrance, albeit a narrow one. Flanking the two sets of double doors that led into the playhouse were two columns called caryatides. Carved in the shape of figures meant to represent "Comedy" and "Song," they defined the Liberty as a house for light entertainment. At the top of the facade was a relief carving of the famous Liberty Bell surmounted by an American eagle with its wings spread wide. Inside, the box office was located in a thirty-foot vestibule treated in old gold and aluminum and covered by a huge oval dome. Embossed leather doors opened into a larger interior foyer. This fifty-foot lobby, decorated in old gold, amber, and ivory, featured a wide staircase to the two balconies and gave access to another promenade behind the orchestra seats. The patriotic theme of the exterior was carried over into the proscenium arch and boxes. Gold eagles and Liberty Bells gleamed high on each side of the theatre, framed by ivory-colored decorative carvings, soft amber walls, and crowned by a Colonial-style ceiling dome. Downstairs, two different lounges provided conveniences for patrons. Ladies could retire in very feminine rooms decorated with green, ivory, and gold pansy designs, while gentlemen enjoyed the masculine surroundings of weathered oak and Spanish leather. Many popular plays and musicals had modest runs at the Liberty during its first two decades, but the premiere attraction and the musical that followed it were not among them. The comedy team of Gus and Max Rogers opened the Liberty Theatre on 14 October 1904 with a musical farce *The Rogers Brothers in Paris*. When their visa expired a month later, George M. Cohan took over the Liberty stage with his new musical *Little Johnny Jones.* It too was unable to find a sizeable audience and closed by February. Some of the theatre's more viable productions included *Polly of the Circus* in 1907 and the 1912 drama *Milestones*. Frank Craven and Ruth Donnelly starred in 351 performances of the 1917 musical *Going Up,* George White presented an early edition of his revue *Scandals* the following year, and Cole Porter contributed the music to *Hitchy-Koo of 1919.* Kern, Kaufman, Cohan, and Gershwin created a series of memorable shows that kept the Liberty's lights blazing in the twenties. The decade began with a five-month hit by Jerome Kern called *The Night Boat.* In 1921 George Gershwin scored the latest *George White Scandals*, followed in 1922 by *To The Ladies*, a hit from George S. Kaufman and Marc Connelly. Another "George" opened with a big success that November. *Little Nelly Kelly*, by George M. Cohan, attracted audiences into the summer of 1923. A year later Gershwin returned to the Liberty with one of the decade's landmark musicals. *Lady*

LEFT : Liberty Theatre, 1911. (MCNY)

ABOVE : Liberty Theatre interior, 1904. (AB)

BELOW : By 1989 the Liberty had lost the bell and eagle from its 42nd Street facade. (MH)

Be Good starred Fred and Adele Astaire and introduced such standards as the title song and the syncopated delight "Fascinating Rhythm." It played 184 times. Gershwin's next musical was the Liberty's next hit; *Tip-Toes*, starring Jeannette MacDonald and Queenie Smith, outran *Lady Be Good* by one week. Bill Robinson and Adelaide Hall opened in the smash hit *Blackbirds of 1928* and were also featured in the Liberty's final success, 1930's *Brown Buddies*.

The Liberty's legitimate career ended on March 18, 1933 when *Masks and Faces* closed after a single performance. Like the other theatres on the block, the Liberty screened movies for the next five decades, finally going dark as the redevelopment of 42nd Street began. With little commercial demand for another small, two-balcony playhouse, it was generally accepted that the Liberty would not be restored to theatrical use. But when a decrepit, run-down venue was sought for a limited run of T. S. Eliot's *The Waste Land* in late 1996, the Liberty wound up with it's first theatrical booking in sixty-three years.

During the run of *The Waste Land* the immediate fate of the Liberty was apparently sealed. Final negotiations were announced that would, while preserving many historic architectural elements, transform the theatre into an interactive video arcade for virtual reality and computer games. The plan, however, was put on hold, and in mid-1997 the future of the Liberty is still in question.

OPPOSITE, TOP : Liberty Theatre, 1997. Developers will be required to preserve or restore the grand proscenium entablature, arches, boxes, curtains, and exteriors on both 42nd and 43rd Streets. (NvH)

OPPOSITE, BOTTOM : The 1,054 seat Liberty Theatre auditorium viewed from stage left in 1997. (NvH)

THE HACKETT THEATER

GRACE GEORGE

HACKETT THEATER
RETURN OF
GRACE GEORGE
A WOMAN'S WAY

GRACE GEORGE

LEW M. FIELDS THEATRE

254 WEST 42ND STREET ALBERT WESTOVER, 1904

In 1904 the comedy team of Joe Weber and Lew Fields closed their famous 29th Street music hall after eight smash years. It would be another nine years before the Shuberts gave them a new theatre on 44th Street. In the interim the comedians found themselves at the Victoria in the employ of Oscar Hammerstein. There they were such a success that Fields, on his own, was able to form a stock company and lease from Hammerstein a new theatre on 42nd Street for his own productions. Financed by the huge profits of his vaudeville complex down the street, the Lew M. Fields Theatre was Hammerstein's eighth playhouse in Manhattan. Like his Republic Theatre, also on 42nd Street, the Fields had a small seating capacity (770) and a tiny lobby, with the last row of orchestra seats directly inside the door. The most striking feature of the interior was the tier of boxes on each side of the proscenium. A total of twenty private boxes flanked the arch, which framed a small but well-appointed stage. (Curiously, Hammerstein had planned for a larger structure, having poured a foundation adequate for a building taller than the Fields' three stories. Yet when the smaller theatre neared completion, Hammerstein had to acquire a structure to the east to provide dressing room space.) The year before the Fields was built a fire at Chicago's Iroquois Theatre had resulted in a tragic loss of life. Thereafter theatre owners took special care to alert a nervous public to the safety features of their playhouses. Hammerstein was no exception. He took great pride in a device of his own invention which he installed in the Fields. "The hundreds of pipes composing the gridiron are converted into an immense system of flood pipes," wrote *The New York Dramatic Mirror* in 1904, "which from their height of seventy feet above the stage floor can be made to liberate a deluge of water in which no flame can live. Simply by pulling a chain on the stage the valves of the two roof tanks, each containing 5,000 gallons of water, are opened and the flood pours down the side walls of the house and thoroughly drenches every other portion of the stage." The Lew M. Fields opened with a hit on 5 December 1904. *It Happened in Nordland,* with music by Victor Herbert and starring Fields himself, ran five months. Despite this early success, however, Fields turned over his playhouse after less than two years to producer/actor James K. Hackett, who renamed it after himself. As the Hackett it enjoyed a number of popular plays, highlighted by the eight-month run of *The Chorus Lady* during the 1906-07 season. In 1911 William B. Harris gained control of the theatre, and once again it had a new name. The building was less successful as the Harris than in other incarnations, but it did manage to attract audiences with *Maggie Pepper* and *The Riddle,* although 1916's *Under Sentence* flopped despite having Edward G. Robinson, Thomas Mitchell, and Frank Morgan in its cast.

LEFT : Lew M. Fields' Theatre was managed by producer/actor James Hackett for five years beginning in 1906. This view dates from 1909. (LC)

ABOVE : In 1990 the theatre, stripped of all exterior and interior decoration, stands converted into shops. (NvH)

The Harris became the Frazee when producer H. H. Frazee opened *The Woman of Bronze* there in 1920. The following year *Dulcy*, starring Lynn Fontanne, Elliott Nugent, and Howard Lindsay, gave George S. Kaufman and Marc Connelly their first Broadway hit. When *Dulcy* closed in 1922, no successes followed, and Frazee lost the theatre two years later. Conjuring up images of a famous nineteenth-century New York City playhouse, the theatre reopened as Wallack's in 1924. *Shipwrecked*, its initial production, foundered after only thirty-one performances. The next year Shirley Booth appeared twice, first in *Hell's Bells* with Humphrey Bogart, and later in *Laff That Off*, a 262-performance hit.

Find the Fox, the theatre's sixth straight flop, ended the Wallack's legitimate career in 1930. The theatre managers closed the dressing rooms, installed a screen, and permanently turned their attention to movies. In 1940 the small house was renamed the Anco and drastically remodeled. The facade was removed, the boxes torn out, the stage sealed, and the two balconies combined into one. Stripped of its character and dignity, the theatre spiraled into oblivion, becoming 42nd Street's least attractive grind house. The final blow was administered in 1988 when the interior was gutted to the bare brick walls and converted into retail space. Located next to the parking lot where the American Theatre once stood, the structure is slated to be demolished in the redevelopment of 42nd Street.

ABOVE : The most striking features of the Lew M. Fields Theatre were the tiers of proscenium boxes that flanked the stage. (LC)

COLONIAL THEATRE

1887 Broadway at 62nd Street George Keister, 1905

The opening of the Colonial Music Hall in 1905 signaled the continued northward expansion of the New York theatrical district. While the vast majority of Times Square theatres were not even on the drawing boards yet, builders Fred Thompson and Elmer Dundy gambled their solvency on a new playhouse for the "Hell's Kitchen" neighborhood of Broadway and 62nd Street. As builders of the New York Hippodrome and Coney Island's Luna Park, they had experience constructing places of entertainment for the popular taste. Their Colonial Music Hall would offer musicals and vaudeville to the residents of the new apartments of upper Broadway.

The Colonial's premiere on 8 February 1905 was an uneventful success. *A Duel in the Snow,* a British pantomime, and a one-act musical called *The Athletic Girl* shared a variety line-up which featured a certain Professor Carl wrestling a trained Russian bear. Other performers in the Colonial's early history were Victor Moore, Lily Langtry, and Edna Aug, who was billed as "a really clever singing comedian."

The theatre itself was modeled after an English music hall. Decorated in bright red, gray, and watered silks, the auditorium was wide although relatively shallow, allowing the balconies to be close to the stage. Ushers wore red and gold uniforms, and Japanese girls served refreshments in a tea room at the rear of the balcony. The house was one of the few New York theatres with frontage on three different streets. The main entrance, with its Federalist facade, was on Broadway. The performers entered from 62nd Street, and the stage loading dock opened onto Columbus Avenue. Inside, there were seats for 647 patrons in the orchestra, 361 in the balcony, and 257 in the gallery. "The new theatre is commodious and comfortable," wrote *The New York Times,* "is handsomely decorated, and promises to be a popular place of amusement for persons who enjoy frothy entertainment."

Two months after the Colonial Music Hall opened, Thompson and Dundy sold the house to Percy Williams, who had made a fortune some years earlier running thirty medicine shows. Williams, now a vaudeville producer, eliminated all of the more "legitimate" entertainment from the bill. Gone were the pantomimes, musicals, and even part of the theatre's name. From now on, as far as Williams was concerned, the Colonial Theatre would be strictly the home of high-class vaudeville.

As the population of the neighborhood increased, so did the size and loyalty of the Colonial's audience. All sections of the theatre cheered their favorite performers, but the more raucous gallery patrons had a notorious method of criticism for acts deserving the hook. They would send down a hail of pennies at the actors thirty feet below, often with deadly accuracy and always without mercy. The tossing would end only when the unfortunate targets left the stage.

Vaudeville was the Colonial's main attraction for the next twenty years. In 1912 B.F. Keith took over the management of the house, changing the name to Keith's Colonial. Five years later E.F. Albee leased the theatre, renovated its interior, and incorporated it into his vaudeville chain as the New Colonial with a bill starring Fred and Adele Astaire.

ABOVE : Colonial proscenium, 1905. (LC)

Musical comedy took over the Colonial in the early twenties with the booking of all-black shows deemed unsuitable for mainstream Broadway theatres. The first of these, 1923's *Runnin' Wild*, introduced a dance that would become the signature of the Jazz Age: The Charleston. Other entertainments on the Colonial stage included *The Chocolate Dandies* by Noble Sissle and Eubie Blake, which played 96 times in 1924, and *Lucky Sambo*, an unlucky flop in 1925. That same year actor Walter Hampden leased the house for personal productions of classic repertory and Shakespeare. Stars like Ethel Barrymore and Maxine Elliott appeared at the renamed Hampden's Theatre in productions of *Hamlet, The Merchant of Venice,* and *Cyrano de Bergerac*. The theatre was finally legitimate as presumably none of these shows featured Russian bear wrestling.

After six seasons Hampden called it quits and relinquished his theatre to the RKO chain. Once again known as the Colonial, it became just another neighborhood movie theatre, grinding out the double features twenty hours a day. In 1956 NBC acquired it from RKO for use as a television studio. In the mid-sixties, after most production moved to the west coast, NBC sold the lease to competing ABC. Their game and talk shows kept the Colonial busy through 1971. **B**y this time the theatre's neighborhood had greatly improved, primarily due to the construction of Lincoln Center directly behind it. When the house was offered for sale for $1.5 million, it was snapped up by oil heiress Rebekah Harkness as the Broadway home for her ballet troupe. A two-year, $5 million restoration followed. When the Harkness Theatre opened in 1974 no critic could argue with the simplistic beauty of the original Federalist facade, or the welcome innovation of the multi-layered stage floor designed specifically for dance. Some, however, thought that the only thing missing from the new decor of powder-blue velvet walls, crystal chandeliers, and powder-blue Louis XIV chairs, was taste. But virtually all critics were appalled by "Homage to Terpsichore," the ultra-realistic proscenium mural drawn from nude photographs of Harkness' dancers in a variety of balletic poses. "Flamboyant," "ugly," "nasty," and "vulgar" were a few of words they used to describe the work. **T**he Harkness Ballet's brief two-week season in New York was not a success, and the theatre remained dark for

BELOW : As the Harkness Theatre, 1974. (NvH)

most of the next year. After running up a $3.5 million deficit, Harkness disbanded her dance troupe and offered the theatre for legitimate bookings. There were not a lot of takers; two weeks of John Houseman's The Acting Company in 1975, a month of Robert Morse in the musical *So Long, 174th Street* the following year. In 1977 the house hit bottom with a booking that recalled the shows of the early twenties. *Ipi-Tombi,* a South African revue featuring native songs and topless tribal dances, was picketed during its brief run. After *Ipi-Tombi* closed, Harkness, no longer able or willing to meet the theatre's annual expenses of $450,000, put the house on the block. In five years she had put over $11 million into her dream theatre. She sold it for one-tenth that amount. In the summer of 1977, after the seats, carpets, chandeliers, and even the mural were auctioned off, the grand old Colonial Theatre was demolished and replaced by condominiums and a public space called the Harkness Atrium.

TOP : Proscenium box, 1973. (NvH)
BOTTOM : Interior during 1973 renovation. (NvH)

THE HIPPODROME

SIXTH AVENUE BETWEEN 43RD & 44TH STREETS J.H. MORGAN, 1905

Two men, one an architect and dreamer from Ohio, the other a promoter and politician from Nebraska, joined forces in 1901 to create a startling new attraction at the Pan American Exposition in Buffalo. "A Trip to the Moon" was the smash hit of the amusement park, and its success was repeated the following year at Coney Island. Soon Frederic Thompson, the dreamer, and Elmer S. Dundy, the promoter, attracted the attention of John W. Gates, a gambler-financier nicknamed "Bet-A-Million." The first result of the Thompson-Dundy-Gates partnership was Luna Park, another wildly successful Coney Island amusement center. Gates had indeed bet a million on it, and his return was rich. Now he wanted bigger risks, bigger profits. He wanted Broadway. **T**he place of amusement that Thompson and Dundy envisioned would be the largest, most spectacular theatre ever built. It would seat more people (5,200) more times per week (14) to watch more performers (1,000, give or take a few horses and elephants) on a stage twelve times bigger than a regular Broadway house. Patterned after the indoor circuses of Europe, the one-and-a-half million dollar Hippodrome opened on 12 April 1905. **T**owering out of the shadows cast by the Sixth Avenue elevated subway, the Hippodrome stretched the entire blockfront between 43rd and 44th streets. Oak trim, plaster-panelled ceilings, and floor mosaics decorated the twin cafes on either side of the marble lobby. Walking past the great curved box offices and the stairways leading to the balconies, patrons entered a block-wide promenade. The outer side of the promenade was lined with mirrors between marble pillars; the inner side led to promenade boxes and to the great auditorium, which was not overdecorated. "Our idea is to place the fancy decorations back of the orchestra and balconies, in the cafe, smoking rooms, and promenades," said Thompson in an interview with the *New York Telegram*. "We do this in order to lend more splendor to the scenic effects on the stage." **T**he auditorium, in spite of Thompson's determination to keep it simple, was not exactly a black box. An anonymous writer in the Hippodrome's souvenier programme described the interior:

> **66** The chief ornamentation consists of great and golden elephant heads, with silvered trappings, and these are studded with electric lights of which there are just a few less than 8,000 from the entrance to the lobby to the dome. On either side of the stage are boxes of various seating capacities, some of them holding forty persons and arranged for parties. Above is the wide sweeping balcony, the front of which is lined with loges, where smoking is permitted. A second balcony stretches out from above. On the mezzanine floor are attractive lounging rooms known as 'The Jungles' where between scenes and during performances visitors find the comfort and attraction of lounging chairs and cozy corners for a chat, a rest and refreshments. **99**

The true wonders of the Hippodrome were found on its stage, which was divided in two parts by a golden proscenium forty feet high and ninety-six feet wide. At sixty feet, the front apron was ten feet deeper than the upstage area and large enough to sup-

ABOVE : B.F. Keith took over the Hippodrome in 1923 and remodeled it into a vaudeville house. (LC)

port two full-sized circus rings. Supported by hydraulic pistons, the apron could be lowered twelve feet and flooded by three centrifugal pumps discharging 8,000 gallons of water per minute. Every possible aquatic effect, from white-water rapids to tidal ocean bay, could be created in the famous Hippodrome tank. The theatre's hydraulic system also enabled a 5,000 square foot section of the stage behind the proscenium to be raised a maximum of eight feet. The unique stage mechanics of the Hippodrome continued in the wings that ran behind the curving auditorium walls. The theatre had no practical fly space, requiring all scenery to move into position from off stage left or right. Attached to the gridiron were four concentric tracks which extended deep into each wing. Electric motors moved entire set pieces on and off along these tracks, eliminating the need to fly any of the massive scenery. Upstage of each wing stood five stories of dressing rooms, and in the basement were stables for the Hippodrome's circus animals and forty horses. The sheer magnitude and novelty of the Hippodrome ensured the success of it's opening double bill, *A Yankee Circus on Mars* and *Andersonville*. The four-hour premiere came off without a hitch, despite the fact that the two productions featured 280 chorus girls, 480 "soldiers," a parade of giant cars driven by elephants, an equestrienne ballet, high-wire acrobatics, and a cavalry charge through a lake. It was a spectacle unlike any ever seen, and the critics were ecstatic. Audiences clamored for tickets, propelling the shows into a 120-performance run. The Hippodrome's second spectacular, *A Society Circus,* opened on 14 December 1905 to raves. "Could anything more be said to show just what this new spectacle is?" wrote the *Evening Telegram.* "In every way it is the biggest and best thing of its kind ever presented in America." The Hippodrome was here to stay. With *A Society Circus* heading towards a record run of nearly 600 performances, Thompson and Dundy once again proved themselves to be two of the theatre's greatest showmen. They were not, however, the theatre's greatest businessmen. In spite of all the rave reviews and demand for tickets, the Hippodrome was actually in serious financial trouble. It cost $6,000 a day just to break even, not to mention paying back any portion of the huge production costs. "Bet-A-Million" Gates liked to gamble, but he wanted better odds than Thompson and

Dundy offered. As the financial backer of the theatre Gates had the final say, and in 1906 he said it. Thompson and Dundy were fired.

Gates turned the Hippodrome over to Lee and J.J. Shubert, who continued to produce the type of spectaculars that made the theatre famous. With a lower admission charge ($1.50) and tighter budget controls, the Hippodrome was soon turning over a tidy weekly profit of $18,000.

ABOVE : Original auditorium, 1918. Nearly seven thousand attend a Sunday night concert by John McCormack. (TM)

During the tenure of the Shubert's first show, *Neptune's Daughter*, the vast water tank was used for an effect that remained a mystery for years. At the finale of the show the chorus marched into the waters, not to resurface until the next performance. Audiences marvelled at the Vanishing Pool, and once again the Hippodrome was the talk of the town. (The secret of the Vanishing Pool was actually quite simple. An elongated diving bell led from the bottom of the tank into the wings. The air trapped in the bell allowed the wet actors to breathe while making a hidden underwater exit). **F**or the next nine years the Hippodrome stage presented auto races, baseball games, flying dirigibles, earthquakes, the Civil War, and the Crusades, all in the guise of musical spectacles. In 1915, after mounting an unsuccessful legitimate production of *HMS Pinafore* and a short-lived circus called *Mammoth Midwinter Circus Supreme*, the Shuberts, feeling the novelty of the Hip-

ABOVE : The last show to play the Hippodrome, 1935. (YL)

podrome had worn off, tried vaudeville and movies before turning the house over to producer Charles Dillingham. **D**ubbed "a national institution" by its new manager, the Hippodrome accommodated eight years of Dillingham's production, including *Hip-Hip-Hooray* and *The Big Show*. His efforts peaked in the 1922 high-flying revue, *Better Times.*

98

ABOVE : Thomas W. Lamb eliminated the famous tanks in favor of 400 more seats when he redesigned the auditorium in 1923. (AB)

Performed more than 400 times, the show was considered by many critics to be the best of the classic Hippodrome extravaganzas. It was also the last. **D**illingham left the Hippodrome in 1923, the same year that a realty company (owners of the property following Gates' death) hoped to replace it with the world's largest hotel. Instead, the house was leased to the Keith-Albee chain for use as a vaudeville theatre. The conversion to vaudeville cost the Hippodrome many of its unique features. Gone were its apron, water tank, hydraulic lifts, and even its wide proscenium. When RKO bought the property in 1925 first-run films played along with the vaudeville acts, but within a few years competition from the newer and more elegant movie palaces proved to be too great. RKO sold the theatre in 1929. **W**hen RKO moved out, Morris Gest moved in to produce the religious epic *The Passion Play.* A pale reminder of the theatre's earlier glories, it ran only five weeks. With the exception of an occasional booking of popular-priced opera, the Hippodrome stood vacant for the next five years. **I**n 1935 a showman in the tradition of Thompson and Dundy brought the Hippodrome back to life. Billy Rose thought the dusty old theatre would be the perfect place for his production of Rodgers and Hart's circus musical *Jumbo,* starring Jimmy Durante and directed by George Abbott. The auditorium was gutted and rebuilt as an actual circus arena, with the action staged in a giant ring. Following six months of rehearsals and nine postponements, *Jumbo* opened on 16 November to favorable reviews. Even without its Vanishing Pool, however, the Hippodrome was a costly theatre to operate. *Jumbo* managed a five month run, closing in the spring of 1936 $160,000 in the red. **T**he Hippodrome had outlived its purpose. Too expensive, too big, and too far east for producers to risk booking, the old brick building housed boxing, wrestling, movies, jai alai, and even an evangelist in its final days. In 1939 the Hippodrome was torn down, but its site remained vacant for thirteen years. Finally, in 1952 ground was broken for an office building and parking structure. Promoted as the world's largest, it is called the Hippodrome Garage.

ABOVE : Children were kept occupied in the basement "Toyland" while parents watched the vaudeville acts upstairs. (AB)

ASTOR THEATRE

1537 BROADWAY AT 45TH STREET GEORGE KEISTER, 1906

When the producing team of Wagenhals and Kemper built the Astor Theatre in 1906, the Times Square area was in the midst of a construction boom. The Astor was the tenth new playhouse to open in six years, and for two decades it would be considered one of Broadway's best. **T**he Astor's long history began with a trio of false starts. A problem with water pressure in a backstage fire pipe caused the opening to be delayed three times. In the final instance, over 1,500 people were asked to clear the house by the fire marshal. When the Astor finally received a permit to open, it was noted that last minute work was not restricted to the plumbing. "The walls were still damp," wrote *The New York Dramatic Mirror,* "and there was a distinct odor of fresh plaster." **L**ocated on the prime northwest corner of Broadway and 45th Street, the Astor was decorated in a simple, neo-Grecian style. The proscenium arch and three bronze lamps hanging directly in front of it were patterned after relics from ancient Athens. Twelve rectangular boxes framed the arch, the severity of their stone construction eased by classic gold ornaments and screenwork friezes. A large globe chandelier illuminated the dark red velvet stage curtain and wall hangings and provided light fo patrons in the orchestra and two balconies. Backstage there were dressing rooms for sixty performers. **F**rom its first attraction, *A Midsummer Night's Dream* starring Annie Russell and John Bunny, the Astor was in demand with both producers and playgoers. Among the Astor's noteworthy attractions during its first few years was the English comic opera *Tom Jones* in 1908 and Douglas Fairbanks, Sr. in the 1912 comedy *Hawthorne of the USA.* This latter show was the first presented by the theatre's new managers George M. Cohan and Sam Harris, who acquired a ten-year lease from Wagenhals and Kemper. The lease specified that the Astor continue to be a playhouse of the first class, retaining its prices and its name. A brief deviation to present the movie *Quo Vadis?* in 1913 notwithstanding, Cohan and Harris were true to their contract. Under their management the Astor had its biggest hits. *Seven Keys to Baldpate, Hello Broadway!,* and *Hit-the-Trail Holliday* kept the house packed through 1916.

That same year Cohan and Harris withdrew to manage their other New York theatres after the Shubert brothers offered a large premium for the Astor lease. During the next few years the theatre's presentations included *Why Marry?,* the first Pulitzer Prize-winning drama, Jerome Kern's tuneful *Rock-A-Bye Baby,* the Shubert revue *Artists and Models,* and George Gershwin's *Sweet Little Devil,* as well as a few motion pictures. Following the eleven-week run of the musical *June Days* in 1925, the Astor permanently gave up legitimate attractions for motion pictures, a policy that continued for fifty years. **A**s the primary Broadway showcase for MGM films, the Astor passed the following three decades with a steady stream of movie hits. In 1959 a million dollar "modernization" stripped the theatre of all architectural ornamentation. A single mezzanine replaced the two balconies and boxes, the stage was removed and proscenium arch rebuilt to accommodate a curved wall-to-wall screen. The orchestra seating area was expanded, a large oil-on-canvas mural titled "New York Summer

LEFT : Astor Theatre exterior (with Wagenhals and Kemper), northwest corner of Broadway and 45th Street, 1909. (HC)

Night" replaced the red velvet wall panels, and the lobby and marquee were redesigned with a bronze and marble motif.

The Astor continued to present movies until 1972, when mechanical problems with the air-conditioning closed the 66 year-old theatre. Assembled with the adjoining Victoria, Helen Hayes, Morosco, and Bijou the-

ABOVE : The Astor's three unique lantern chandeliers, 1906. (LOC)

atres as the site of a new office tower, demolition was slated to begin almost immediately following its closing. But a glut of empty office space delayed the plans, and the razing was cancelled. Nevertheless, the Astor's seats were removed. With the exception of infrequent use as retail space, the auditorium and lobby remained empty and closed for a decade. In 1982, after a ten-year preservation effort failed, the five theatres were demolished. Today, a skyscraper hotel, containing New York's newest legitimate theatre, towers on the site of the Astor and its neighbors.

ABOVE : In 1973 the Astor reopened as a discount art gallery. (NvH)

LEFT : Astor interior, 1906. (LOC)

BELOW : The Astor following its 1959 "modernization" as a state-of-the-art movie theatre. (LC)

GAIETY THEATRE

1547 BROADWAY AT 46TH STREET HERTS & TALLANT, 1908

When a 1982 demolition team ripped into the 46th Street facade of the old Gaiety Theatre, they exposed the worn out remains of a playhouse built to present the best comedy Broadway could offer. But an instant later the theatre had the last laugh as its balcony and roof collapsed into the street, blocking traffic for two days. Seventy-four years before tons of brick and plaster cascaded into West 46th Street, the Gaiety Theatre had opened to glowing reviews. Because of its slender proportions, it was dubbed a "bandbox" by critics who were impressed by its beauty and, despite two balconies and nearly a thousand seats, its intimacy. After attending the first night festivities, one anonymous writer described the new theatre in *The New York Telegraph:*

> 66 To begin with the Gaiety is not pretentious except in quality. The auditorium is small, as the auditorium in every comedy house should be, according to an expert who gives his opinion on the programme. A joke or a clever line goes twice as well when delivered at short range as when delivered at a distance.
>
> The decorations of the little playhouse which is to become the home of comedy are in Louis XV style, and there is an imposing entrance on the 46th Street side as well as one on Broadway. A broad foyer on the 46th Street side contributes to the convenience and comfort of patrons.
>
> The color scheme is a delight to the eye, being beautiful and soft in Sevres blue, French gray, and old gold effectively blended. The side walls, covered with delicate gray silk, are embossed with a comic mask, surmounted with the laureled monogram, 'G.T.'—Gaiety Theatre.
>
> The same blue-gray and old gold prevail in the frescoing of the proscenium arch and the two large proscenium boxes. The boxes are roomy, and off one of them is a reception parlor, where a theatre party may retire between acts and enjoy themselves in an atmosphere as exclusive as that of their own homes. Exquisite tapestries are used throughout the house for mural effects. The orchestra chairs, covered with steel-gray leather, are pleasing to the eye and they are arranged with a view to comfort rather than with a view to the utilization of every square inch of space. The dome chandelier is a huge twelve-pointed star, surrounded with circular lamps studded with electric lights. 77

The Gaiety was owned by the producing team of Klaw and Erlanger, who managed the house along with George M. Cohan and his partner Sam Harris. Wanting to open their house with a proven hit, they revived Cohan's musical *The Yankee Prince,* featuring the entire Cohan family. The single-week engagement of the show packed the house and started the Gaiety off on the road to success. In the two decades that followed the Gaiety earned a reputation as a house of hits. Helen Hayes, John Barrymore, and Douglas Fairbanks were audience favorites, as was John Golden's 1918 comedy *Lightnin',* which was the first Broadway show to give more than one thousand performances. Although the Gaiety was in constant demand as a house for plays, its relatively shallow stage limited its use for musical productions. Only five played the house, including the opening show, two revues, and George Gershwin's *Tell Me More,* which ran twelve weeks in 1925. Oddly enough, the original title of the Gershwin show, *My Fair Lady,* was dropped for being uncommercial.

Movies took over the Gaiety in 1926 for five years, after which the house returned to comedies with *Peter Pan Flies High* in 1931 and John Anderson's *Collision* in

ABOVE : Gaiety interior, 1908. (AB)

1932. Both shows flopped, and the house permanently left the legitimate scene.

Much to the delight of its male patrons, and to the dismay of Mayor Fiorello LaGuardia, the Gaiety turned to burlesque be-

ABOVE : Gaiety interior, 1908. (AB)

tween movie bookings. As Broadway's premiere bump-and-grind house, the Gaiety presented the superstars of the strip-tease, Ann Corio and Gypsy Rose Lee, plus top comics Bud Abbott and Lou Costello. When La-Guardia finally put a stop to burlesque in 1942, the theatre turned to vaudeville, offering Stepin Fetchit in *Harlem on Broadway*. This policy was short-lived, however, and after rumors of a return to legitimate shows, the Gaiety was renamed the Victoria and leased to the movies. **T**he next forty years were uneventful, the Victoria known more for the gigantic billboard above it than for the films it presented. The house made one final name change in the late seventies when Embassy Theatres dubbed it the Embassy Five, but its days were numbered. The theatre, long forgotten as a legitimate house, was part of the site for a new hotel. Preservationists managed to keep the wreckers away until the spring of 1982. But as soon as their court battles were lost, a block rich in theatre history came down.

ABOVE : Broadway entrance to the Gaiety Theatre, 1908. (AB)

ABOVE : Maxine Elliott's Theatre, 1908. (SA)

MAXINE ELLIOTT'S THEATRE

109 WEST 39TH STREET MARSHALL & FOX, 1908

Actress Maxine Elliott wrote in *Woman's Home Companion,* "For eight years I have cherished consistently—though I am a woman—the dream of building a theatre that should be small and intimate; that should be beautiful and harmonious to the eye in every last detail; that should be comfortable for the spectators, and, behind the scenes, comfortable and humane for every least player in the company . . . Of course," she wrote, "I had to have the assistance of a man!" For support she turned to Lee Shubert, who sold her a small site on West 39th Street in return for a fifty percent interest in the property. After eighteen successful years on New York and London stages, Elliott realized her dream to become one of the only female managers on Broadway. Although her playhouse took only four months to build, Elliott kept her promise to make it as beautiful and comfortable as possible. With the help of Chicago architects Marshall & Fox, she patterned her theatre after Le Petit Trianon at Versailles. Above the main entrance the theatre's name was chiseled into a cornice supported by four Corinthian columns. With the exception of this 39th Street facade, which was covered in Dorset marble, the Elliott's exterior was faced with gray brick trimmed with terra-cotta. English veined marble lined the lobby walls and ceiling, and white Italian marble formed the sweeping staircases leading to the balconies. A broad foyer behind the orchestra seats stretched the entire width of the theatre and led to the lounges and cloakrooms under the lobby. Separated from the auditorium by mouse brown velvet curtains, which were the same color as the theatre's thick carpets, the foyer featured a marble base, an ornamental relief ceiling in old ivory, and side walls covered in gold silk damask. Gold silk also lined the side walls and boxes of the 900-seat auditorium. Two giant columns supporting the proscenium arch were carved from golden-grained Skyros marble, the same material in the railings that separated the orchestra boxes from the rest of the house. Rose garlands decorated both the vaulted ceiling above the proscenium and the large flat dome that crowned the auditorium. A French glass chandelier hung from the center of the old ivory-colored dome and was supplemented throughout the house by old gold lighting fixtures. All the seats were framed in old ivory and upholstered in the same brown velvet used in the house curtain, boxes, and foyer. The appointments behind the footlights were just as sumptuous. All of the dressing rooms boasted carpeting, windows, full-length mirrors, English armchairs, and private bathroom facilities. Elliott's dressing room, directly off stage left, had its own reception area complete with mahogany furniture. The theatre opened with *The Chaperon,* starring Elliott, on 30 December 1908. Critics admired the playhouse but had little use for the play, which lasted six weeks. The first real success came in October 1909 in the form of the morality play *The Passing of the Third Floor Back,* followed a year later by an eight-month run of *The Gamblers.* Although Elliott had been quoted as saying that musicals would never play her theatre, one did manage to appear there for two weeks in 1916. *See America First* would have passed into theatrical obscurity had it not featured the first complete Broadway score by then 24 year-old Cole Porter. More than 14 years later another young talent would attract attention at the Elliott. The play was *Art and Mrs. Bottle*, the actress, Katharine Hepburn.

Over the years many successful shows opened or closed at the Elliott, but few of them stayed for their entire runs. There were exceptions, though, including *The Constant Wife* starring Ethel Barrymore, Jeanne Eagels in *Rain,* Helen Hayes in *Coquette,* and

ABOVE : The orchestra promenade. (SA)

Lillian Hellman's *The Children's Hour,* which broke the house record with 691 performances in 1936. Orson Welles and Joseph Cotten appeared in various productions under the auspices of the Federal Theatre Project, and later the hit comedy *Separate Rooms* began its long run at the Elliott.

ABOVE : Interior, 1908. (SA)

Following the appearance of the Ballet Joos in 1941, the theatre was leased to the Mutual Network for use as a radio studio. CBS christened the building Radio Playhouse No. 5 when that network took over the lease in 1944, and renamed it Studio No. 51 when it was converted to television four years later. As a television studio the Elliott was home to many popular game and variety shows, including the first Ed Sullivan program, *The Toast of the Town.* In 1956 the heirs of Maxine Elliott, who had died at her home on the French Riviera in 1940, sold their share of the theatre to the Shuberts. They in turn sold the entire building to developers, who planned to raze it once CBS' lease expired.

When Maxine Elliott's Theatre opened it was surrounded by some of Broadway's finest theatres. The Casino, Empire, Abbey's, and later the Princess, Nazimova's, and Comedy were all neighbors. By the time CBS closed the theatre in 1959 it was the only Broadway house still standing south of 41st Street, a relic of a bygone era. That era ended when the house was demolished in January 1960.

ABOVE : Box office lobby, 1908. (SA)

ABOVE : Comedy Theatre, 1909. (AB)

COMEDY THEATRE

108 WEST 41ST STREET D.G. MALCOLM, 1909

With the opening of the Comedy Theatre in 1909, the Shubert empire moved one block closer to the square it would eventually dominate. The only playhouse on 41st Street between Broadway and Bryant Park, the Comedy never quite matched the success of the other Shubert theatres; but during its thirty-three years of operation the Comedy more than earned a place in the history of Broadway theatre. Of six theatres under construction in 1909, the Comedy was the most intimate and the most delicate. It presented to 41st Street an exterior of imitation limestone (actually cement) bordering a tapestry of buff-colored brick. A narrow lobby contained the box office and gave access to the rear of the auditorium. The house was shallow and small, its orchestra, balcony, gallery, and boxes totaling only 623 seats. The interior decoration was quite subdued for the era, with ornamental plasterwork used sparingly save for the proscenium arch and box canopy. The smooth walls were painted a light shade of old rose while the carpets and upholstery were colored in a darker shade of the same tone. The cream white of the balconies and boxes added to the warmth of the house as did the silver-gray tones of the proscenium. The theatre's premiere attraction, *The Melting Pot,* a comedy from the pen of Israel Zangwill, kept audiences laughing for four months. Comedian William Collier moved in next, leasing the house for three years. He renamed it Collier's Comedy Theatre, starred in *I'll Be Hanged If I Do,* turned the stage over to Douglas Fairbanks, Sr. for *The Cub,* and sublet the theatre to Cecil B. DeMille for his production of *Speed.* In 1916 the Washington Square Players leased the Comedy for a season. It was in a bit part in their production of *Bushido* that Katharine Cornell made her Broadway debut. The following year the Players gave Eugene O'Neill his first Broadway production when they staged his one-act play *In the Zone* at the Comedy. Although the Players left the Comedy at the start of World War I, they did manage to reunite at a different theatre two years later. They named their new group the Theatre Guild. The next decade saw few memorable plays at the Comedy but many memorable performances, including turns by Humphrey Bogart, Paul Robeson, Holbrook Blinn, Peggy Hopkins, Walter Abel, Leo Carrillo, and Ruth Draper in the first performances of her famous one-woman show. In 1928, in one of the first applications of a new censorship law, the New York district attorney padlocked the Comedy during the run of *Maya.* The wave of protest that followed caused a change in the law. No longer would performers be criminally liable for the content of their roles. Although some critics suggested that actors still be held criminally liable for their performances, everyone agreed that this was a major victory in the battle against censorship in the theatre. Like many of the other theatres throughout the district, the Comedy was a casualty of the stock market crash. It stood in darkness, closed and virtually forgotten, from 1931 to 1935. Reopened by the Metropolitan Players, an amateur group from Newark, the Comedy eventually came to the attention of Orson Welles and John Houseman. They found its intimacy ideal for the season of drama they planned for their group, the Mercury Players. In 1937 Welles and Houseman took over the theatre, renamed it the Mercury, and began rehearsals for their initial offering. When *Julius Caesar* opened that November, New Yorkers saw a modern-dress version that was decidedly anti-fascist. Other Mercury productions followed, but none had the impact of the Shakespeare drama. By the end of the decade Welles, Houseman, and the Mercury Players

ABOVE : Comedy Theatre interior, 1909. (AB)

were conjuring up Martians on the radio.

In 1940 the theatre was renamed the Artef after becoming the fourth Broadway home for the Yiddish Art Players. After some success they abandoned the small playhouse the following year. The victim of size, location, and competition, the Comedy stood empty until the wreckers took over in 1942.

ABOVE : Comedy interior, 1909. (AB)

ABOVE : The New Theatre, Central Park West at
62nd Street, in 1909. (HC)

NEW THEATRE

Unlike many countries of the world, the United States has never had a national theatre. While governments in Europe have supported countless stage companies and their productions, ours has preferred to let theatre remain primarily an independent speculative commercial venture. In the first decade of this century, a group of prominent New Yorkers took it upon themselves to create their version of a national theatre.

The list of names read like a Who's Who of the social elite: John Jacob Astor, Henry Clay Frick, J.P. Morgan, Cornelius Vanderbilt, Harry Payne Whitney. They were the founders of the New Theatre movement, and the goals they established for their playhouse were noble ones. The theatre would be operated solely for the advancement of art and not for commercial gain. All profits from productions, with the exception of a modest interest paid to investors, would be used to create and endow an on-site school for dramatic and musical arts. In 1906 a site away from the commercial lure of Times Square was chosen, and the design competition was announced. The call for entries proposed a theatre that was

" not to be understood in the usual American interpretation of the word; that is, a mere show house where the entire building is given over to the auditorium and the stage. It is intended to conform more nearly to the continental type of theatre in which the auditorium and stage occupy only a moderate portion of the plan, and provision is made for a foyer, grand staircases, ample retiring and cloak rooms, smoking rooms, entrances, circulations and elevators, restaurant, confectioner, florist, and similar accommodations for the public. In its architectural aspect the problem is one that calls not only for a practical solution, but is also one in which the artistic treatment is of paramount importance. "

The founders selected the firm of Carrere & Hastings to design the theatre for the fee of six percent of the estimated $1,700,000 cost of the building (excluding land, stage-fittings, and fees). Their winning plan, based on the founder's precise guidelines, described a building in the Italian Renaissance style. The Indiana limestone exterior covered the entire block between 62nd and 63rd streets. The main pedestrian entrance was from the park side, while the carriage trade used doorways on both side streets. Massive spiral staircases at the theatre's corners led to lobbies that wrapped around each of the auditorium's four levels. Behind the 600 seats on the main floor were the twenty-three Founder's boxes, sold in perpetuity to their occupants for $25,000 apiece. Above them was a shallow mezzanine called "the foyer stalls," and above that the first and second balconies. The total capacity of the driftwood gray and dull Roman gold auditorium was 2,318. The stage of the New Theatre was large and its center section revolved, greatly reducing the time between scenes. The unique fly system funneled shot in and out of counterweight buckets, eliminating the reliance on motors and winches. Backstage, the thirty-eight individual dressing rooms and four chorus rooms could handle the casts of everything from Shakespeare to opera. On top of the main theatre was a roof garden, initially used as rehearsal space, but built to house productions of its own.

The opening of the New Theatre on 8 November 1909 was the social event of the year. It was not, however, the theatrical event it was hoped to be. Both the building and the premiere production, *Antony and Cleopatra,* received mixed reviews. "The theatre itself is a delight to the eye," said *The New York Times,* "even if, as it appeared on the opening night, something yet remains to be accomplished to bring complete satisfaction to the ear." **B**ad acoustics plagued the theatre for its first season, enraging patrons and prompting suggestions for major reconstruction, including removal of the second balcony, lowering the ceiling, relocating the Founder's Boxes to the auditorium sides, extending the remaining balconies forward, and reducing the seating capacity by six hundred. The founders did block off the balcony and half of the boxes, but the public still avoided the playhouse. **B**y the end of the second year, the New Theatre's net losses totaled $400,000. It was obvious that the founder's dream of a national theatre would never be realized in the huge playhouse they had built. Rather than make the necessary interior alterations, they voted to try again from the ground up. They abandoned the uptown location of the New Theatre in favor of a site directly behind the Hotel Astor in the heart of Times Square. Stretching between 44th and 45th Streets, the latest New Theatre would seat 1,200 and share a private roadway with

BELOW : Interior, 1909. (LOC)

the hotel. The site was cleared, but before construction began the founders withdrew, claiming area competition and an inability to find a suitable director for their company. Lee and J.J. Shubert took advantage of the founders' waning interest and purchased the site from them. There they constructed two theatres that stand today, the Shubert and the Booth. The private roadway became known as Shubert Alley. It is ironic that the most altruistic intentions of New York's wealthiest men directly resulted in the creation of the city's commercial theatre center. While all this was happening downtown, uptown the old New Theatre had a brand-new name, the Century, and was available for rent like any other Broadway house. In addition to standard touring musicals and dramatic spectacles, the theatre also booked operas and music hall varieties. In 1916 Florenz Ziegfeld and Charles Dillingham, two of Broadway's top musical producers, joined forces to present a successful revue, *The Century Girl,* with a score by Irving Berlin and Victor Herbert. The sequel, *Miss 1917,* fared less well in spite of Jerome Kern's music and P.G. Wodehouse's sketches. A year later Irving Berlin returned to the Century with the short-lived soldier revue *Yip Yip Yaphank,* which introduced the song "Oh, How I Hate To Get Up In The Morning."

BELOW : Within a few years of opening minor alterations were made to the interior of the New Theatre. Note the change in box and balcony seating and the additions of a dropped ceiling for better acoustics. (LOC)

Control of the theatre next passed into the hands of the Shubert brothers, who made it the home for a series of operettas, including *The Rose of Stamboul, Princess Flavia,* and revivals of *Florodora* and *The Chocolate Soldier.* The Shuberts also took over the Century Roof, which had seen duty as everything from an amateur children's theatre (complete with kid-sized seats) to a cabaret called The Coconut Grove. Under Shubert direction, a number of late-night revues were booked in the 500-seat rooftop playhouse. The most successful of these was *Chauve-Souris,* a Russian vaudeville performed by exiled

ABOVE : The New Theatre's elaborate proscenium. (TH)

members of the Moscow Art Theatre. A memorable night at the Century Roof was the premiere of the fourth edition of *Chauve-Souris,* attended by visiting Russian theatre luminaries Konstantin Stanislovsky and Olga Knipper-Chekov. With the Russians ensconced on the roof, the theatre below gave way to the Germans when Max Reinhardt's breathtaking production of the play *The Miracle* opened in 1923. Designer Norman Bel Geddes transformed the Century's vast auditorium into a Gothic cathedral, and for once acoustics were not a problem; *The Miracle* had no dialogue. As one might guess, the combination of German religious melodramatics and mime also had no profits. By 1926 the Century's days were numbered.

The Times Square theatre boom had doubled the amount of available playhouses, and the inconvenient Century couldn't compete. Its occassional bookings were mostly return engagements of Broadway hits, including *Rain, The Jazz Singer,* and *The Cocoanuts.* The theatre was also still fighting its twenty-year old problem. As late as 1928 stars refused to play the Century for fear of not being heard past the first ten rows. Upstairs, the roof theatre enjoyed one final name change, to the Casino de Paris, and one last hit, the Shubert revue *A Night in Paris.* When this show closed, the character of the roof theatre and its bookings declined. The vaudeville that kept the small house lit for its last few years was indistinguishable from that at any of the city's neighborhood theatres. In October 1929, the Chanin Construction Company acquired the Century Theatre from the Shuberts. A year later, twenty-two years after President Theodore Roosevelt congratulated the founders of the New Theatre on their commitment to the arts, the mammoth building was razed and replaced by the Century Apartments.

ABOVE : The roof garden, 1909. (LOC)

ABOVE : Smaller seats replaced the full size variety when
the roof garden was a children's theatre in 1912. (HC)

63RD STREET MUSIC HALL

22 WEST 63RD STREET THOMAS W. LAMB, 1909•ERWIN ROSSBACH, 1914

Actor Butler Davenport's theatre was to have opened in the winter of 1909 as a home for a new stock company. But after the steel for the stage and balcony had been welded in place financial difficulties overtook the project and the construction of the Davenport Theatre ceased. However, in a combined effort in 1914 the People's Pulpit Association and the International Bible Student's Association managed to complete the building and open it as a 1,024-seat temple for the presentation of Biblical movies and religious lectures. On Christmas Day 1919 the house finally made its debut as a theatre for popular entertainment. Named the 63rd Street Music Hall, it opened with a policy of movies for children. The films flopped, and ten days later the house was dark. Producer John Cort took it over, renamed it Cort's 63rd Street, and christened it on 31 January 1921 with *Mixed Marriage*. But when it moved to a downtown house shortly after the opening the theatre once again became known as the 63rd Street Music Hall. In May of 1921 a musical with a talented black cast was unable to secure a booking in a mainstream Broadway house. Forced to settle for the out-of-the-way theatre on 63rd Street, *Shuffle Along* beat the odds and became the surprise smash hit of the season. For 504 performances audiences cheered the Eubie Blake-Noble Sissle score (featuring hits "I'm Just Wild About Harry" and "Bandanna Days") delivered by new stars Florence Mills and Josephine Baker. *Shuffle Along* made black shows acceptable to white audiences and put the uptown house on the map. After *Shuffle Along* closed in 1922 the theatre was redecorated a brilliant red and gold and renamed for the famous 19th century theatre manager August Daly. But despite all the effort to upgrade the building the cast of *Dolly Jordan* (the first booking at Daly's 63rd Street) was not happy with the theatre. It was felt that Daly's was not the first-class house that had been promised; on opening night loose stage boards banged as actors stepped on them, and the constant ringing of an out-of-order telephone somewhere in the theatre could be heard throughout the play, which was set in the 1700s. The *Dolly Jordan* cast didn't suffer for long, though, as the play folded after its fifth showing. Presumably the problems were corrected before *Liza,* the theatre's second successful black musical, began its 21-week run a month later.

Antoinette Perry, Basil Rathbone, and Mae West appeared at Daly's over the next five years, but there wasn't another run longer than 100 performances until *Keep Shuffling* opened in 1928. Although the show played four hundred fewer times than its predecessor, it did boast a score with contributions by Fats Waller, who was also in the cast. In November of that year Mr. and Mrs. Charles Coburn, a popular acting couple, leased the house for a revival of one of their hits, *The Yellow Jacket*. The theatre's name was changed to the Coburn for the event, which only lasted ten weeks. After a second ill-fated production they withdrew from the house.

LEFT : The 63rd Street Music Hall was known as
the Coburn Theatre in 1928. (NYPL)

The theatre operated under a variety of names during the thirties. As the Recital it presented four showings of *Lady Windermere's Fan* in 1932. That spring the theatre reopened as the Park Lane, and by the end of 1934 it was known as Gilmore's

ABOVE : Exterior, 1936. (GMU)

63rd Street, a home for cut-rate revivals. When the Federal Theatre Project took over in 1936 the theatre was renamed the Experimental. Among its shows were *Chalk Dust, The Path of Flowers,* and the New York premiere of George Bernard Shaw's *On The Rocks.* When the Theatre Project moved out in 1937, the amateur Artef Players moved in for a brief stay. In 1938 the theatre was available again as Daly's 63rd Street, but there were no takers and the house went dark.

After being closed for over two years, producer Alexander H. Cohen leased the house with the intention of establishing a stock company there. He opened *Ghost for Sale* in September 1941, but six performances later it vanished. Daly's, after ten changes of name in thirty years, permanently shuttered. The theatre didn't surface again until 1957 when the long-forgotten house, now at the northern edge of the district, was demolished.

BELOW : As the Experimental Theatre, part of the Federal Theatre Project, in 1936. (GMU)

NAZIMOVA'S 39TH STREET THEATRE

119 WEST 39TH STREET   WILLIAM A. SWASEY, 1910

In an era when great actresses only played great parts, Alla Nazimova was considered a genius. Her interpretations of Ibsen's and Chekov's leading ladies brought her nationwide acclaim. Her managers Lee and J.J. Shubert, to celebrate Nazimova's success (and to insure her fidelity to their firm), dedicated their newest theatre to their popular star.

Nazimova's 39th Street Theatre was one of Broadway's smaller playhouses. From the Italian Renaissance exterior, audiences entered the auditorium through a lobby with marble walls and a gold-finished ceiling. Those with seats in the balconies reached them by staircases off the foyer or by an elevator located at the gallery entrance. The 699-seat interior was decorated in the style of Louis XVI. Plaster fruit garlands and wreaths over a latticed background adorned the ceiling coves while ornamental beams enriched the ceiling itself. Ionic pilasters flanked the four boxes and supported a plaster relief symbolic of the drama. Decorated with silk tapestries, each wall panel was illuminated by a single silk-shaded lamp, with the general lighting coming from four gold sunburst fixtures in the main ceiling. All curtains, carpets, drapes, and upholstery were in shades of old rose, with exposed wood finished in gold. The backstage area featured star dressing rooms behind the boxes and four tiers of additional dressing rooms stage right. Out front were private studios and offices, including those of the Shubert brothers.

As was only appropriate with such an honor, the great Nazimova herself opened the theatre on 18 April 1910 in Henrik Ibsen's *Little Eyolf*. Although the Shuberts were prolific builders and producers, they were not the top managers of the times; that honor was claimed by Henry B. Harris or Charles Frohman. When Frohman offered Nazimova a contract in 1911 she jumped at it, leaving the Shuberts and her theatre behind. Having lost a top star to a competitor, Lee and J.J. removed her name from the marquee. For the next fifteen years the theatre was known as simply the 39th Street.

The 39th Street's intimacy and decor made it a favorite among playgoers, but it was not a very lucky house for producers. The theatre's longest run of thirty-nine weeks was achieved by the play *Scandal*. The aptly-titled *A Little Piece of Fluff* held the record for the shortest run: one performance. Between were modest runs of forgotten plays such as *Believe Me Xantippe*, *Old Lady 31*, *The Unchastened Woman*, and *We Can't Be As Bad As All That*. Although most of the plays at the 39th Street weren't milestones of the theatre, certain stars did shine in them. The roster included Frank Craven, H.B. Warner, Annie Russell, Mrs. Leslie Carter, Marie Dressler, and in the same show, John Barrymore and Douglas Fairbanks.

Following bookings of the South Seas melodrama *White Cargo* and a comedy called *Laff That Off,* the Shuberts closed the 39th Street on 2 January 1926. The brothers had other theatres that were bigger and more centrally located in the district they helped to build. Developer A.E. Lefcourt bought the playhouse, razed it, and constructed a 20-story office building on the site. The pretty little 39th Street Theatre was only sixteen years old when it came down and was the first of the new uptown theatres to fall to the wrecker's ball.

LEFT : 39th Street Theatre, circa 1925. (NYPL)

LEFT : Proscenium boxes, 1910. (AB)

BELOW : Nazimova's auditorium, 1910. (AB)

GEORGE M. COHAN'S THEATRE

1482 Broadway at 43rd Street George Keister, 1911

For the first part of this century, the number one star of the musical comedy stage was author, singer, dancer, producer, and director George M. Cohan. At the peak of his popularity in 1911, it was only fitting that he add "theatre-manager" to his long list of accomplishments. On the southeast corner of Broadway and 43rd Street a twelve-story office structure known as The FitzGerald Building graced Times Square with an elegant white facade of polished granite, limestone, and semi-glazed terra cotta. The ground floor boasted a restaurant and drugstore, plus a sixteen-foot wide lobby leading to George M. Cohan's Theatre, which stood directly behind the building. The facade of the 43rd Street main entrance matched the FitzGerald in color, material, and design. Inside, Cohan's Theatre was less restrained. The long lobby was decorated with murals depicting highlights in the careers of Cohan and his family, most of whom were often his co-stars. Similar murals also adorned the auditorium. Above and beside the proscenium arch, and over the gold and purple boxes were paintings of scenes from some of Cohan's biggest hits, including *Little Johnny Jones, The Yankee Prince,* and *George Washington, Jr.*

The design of the two-balcony, 1,100-seat auditorium was in the early Italian style, with heavy crossbeams dividing the ceiling into square panels. Soft gray marble and low-toned bronze formed the wainscoting. In addition to the murals, sections of the walls were covered with silk dyed in the latest Paris tint, Tyrian purple, and bordered with Sheffield silver. The drop curtain matched the silk hangings and featured in its center a large monogrammed medallion. Behind the scenes, the dressing rooms could accommodate a cast of one hundred. In the wings there was a special alcove for the electrician's switchboard, and under the large stage a carpeted greenroom doubled as a rehearsal hall. Cohan's Theatre opened with the transfer from the Gaiety of a Cohan hit, *Get-Rich-Quick Wallingford.* This was followed by another Cohan smash, *The Little Millionaire,* and late in 1912 by a third, *Broadway Jones.* An outside booking the following year became the long-run champ at Cohan's; *Potash & Perlmutter,* a play based on stories in the *Saturday Evening Post,* chalked up 441 performances. The theatre's next offering, *It Pays To Advertise,* entertained audiences for nearly a year.

Despite the early successes, George M. Cohan's Theatre attracted its share of flops, and by 1923 ticket sales from Sunday night movie screenings helped pay the mortgage. But using a legit house on its dark night for lectures or films was a common practice in the twenties, and on the whole the theatre's second decade passed uneventfully. . . well, almost. Early on the cold morning of 8 March 1926, there was a knock on the 43rd Street stage door of Cohan's Theatre. The night watchman, nearing the end of his shift, responded, thinking only that perhaps the day crew was early. When he opened the door, this thought was erased from his mind by the pain of hard steel pressed against his temple. "Take us to the safe, or I'll blow your head off," said one of two gunmen. The terrified guard led the robbers to

the house manager's office while three other members of the gang grabbed the custodial staff. **R**ope and telephone wire cut into the wrists of the Cohan employees as they were tied to wooden chairs in the office. "Hurray up," ordered the leader, "let's crack the safe and get out of here." Minutes seemed like hours as the

ABOVE : Broadway entrance to the theatre, 1915. (NYHS)

OPPOSITE PAGE : 43rd Street facade, 1911. (MCNY)

metal of the safe groaned under the pressure of the burglar's "can opener." Finally, the heavy door swung open and the contents of the safe were revealed to all. "Hey," cried the boss, "there's nothing in here but a stack of these lousy programs!" Angrily they left the theatre, but not before they spat in the faces of their helpless victims, leaving them generally uninjured but thoroughly revolted.

ABOVE : Auditorium, 1911. (AB)

ABOVE : Broadway entrance, 1929. (TH)

Cohan's Theatre ushered in the thirties with a black revue, *Change Your Luck,* featuring Alberta Hunter, and a white revue, *Shoot the Works,* with George Murphy and Imogene Coca. Both were duds. A few more flops followed, and after an 11-week run of the operetta *The DuBarry* in 1932, George M. Cohan's Theatre gave its final regards to Broadway and called it quits as a legitimate house. Embracing the motion picture as its primary source of income, the theatre struggled for six years against the nearby competition (the Roxy, Rialto, Paramount, State, Rivoli, Strand, among others) for its share of the movie audience. It was a losing battle, though, and by 1938 both Cohan's and The FitzGerald building were considered Broadway's whitest elephants. The New York State Life Insurance Company bought the properties at auction for the nominal bid of $100,000. Demolition took about eight weeks, and in early 1939 tax-paying stores were erected on the site.

VIEWS OF THE INTERIOR OF GEORGE M. COHAN'S NEW THEATRE
NEW YORK CITY.

ABOVE : Cohan himself in 1911, surrounded by views of his theatre. (HC)

PLAYHOUSE THEATRE

137 West 48th Street · Charles A. Rich, 1911

The Playhouse was the first theatre to open on 48th Street and the first of two theatres built on that avenue by producer William A. Brady. Under his guidance it survived two world wars, prohibition, and the depression with its comfortable stage, charming decor, and reputation as a "house of hits" intact. From the start the five-story facade of the Playhouse and its rich interior were admired by audiences and critics. Many publications of the day described Broadway's newest theatre, but none was as thorough as *The New York Commercial Advertiser:*

> The building is constructed of brick, with stone facings, and is a combination of the French and Colonial styles of architecture. The front of the building is imposing and almost severe, but this severity is relieved by stone carvings of comedy and tragedy set in the wall, marble window medallions, a flowered frieze, and other ornaments of trimmed stone.
>
> The main entrance is under a canopy of steel and glass, and leads through oaken doors, set in diamond glass, into the lobby, which is enclosed in white marble. The main entrance as well as the entrances leading to the gallery and studios are flanked by brick posts, surmounted with stone urns, and joined by a novel grilled iron fence.
>
> The interior of the house gives the impression of cosy compactness. All parts of the house, including the balcony and gallery, are brought very near to the stage, so that audience and players will be in close sympathy. The loss of depth in obtaining this desirable result is compensated for by the extreme width of the auditorium. The boxes are set back, although they are large and roomy, and there is no interference with the line of vision. There is a free view of the stage from every part of the house. The decorations are in deep red, gold, and brown, with brown carpets and blue draperies.
>
> The stage of The Playhouse is large and fitted with every appliance known to modern stage craft. It can be utilized for the simple stage settings of a parlor comedy or the intricate stage paraphernalia of a spectacle . . . Especial attention has also been given to the dressing rooms for the players. They are cosy and comfortable, steam heated and well ventilated, and furnished with every convenience. The star dressing rooms have bathrooms attached.

Brady's offices occupied the entire fourth floor of the 900-seat theatre, while the top floor of the building, with its large, sloping windows, was occupied by studios. The Playhouse opened on 15 April 1911 with a comedy called *Sauce For The Goose* starring Brady's wife, Grace George. The show flopped, however, and was quickly replaced with *Over Night,* which was moved from the Hackett. That same year Douglas Fairbanks appeared as *A Gentleman of Leisure,* and George Broadhurst's *Bought and Paid For* began its smash run of 431 performances. The next twenty years were highlighted by another 400-plus winner, *The Man Who Came*

LEFT : The Playhouse during the 1921–22 season. (LC)

135

ABOVE : The Playhouse interior, 1911. (LC)

Back in 1917, Elmer Rice's 1929 Pulitzer champ *Street Scene,* plus acclaimed performances in between by the likes of Edward G. Robinson, Henry Hull, Lionel Atwell, Howard Lindsay, and many others. Despite booking sixteen flops in a row, Brady was one of the very few owners who did not lose his theatre in the depression that followed 1929's stock market crash. His tenacity paid off in 1935 with the premiere of another huge success, *Three Men on a Horse*, starring Shirley Booth and Sam Levene. Appearances by Tallulah Bankhead, Laurette Taylor, and Vincent Price closed out the decade. Following Brady's death in 1944 at the age of eighty-one, control of the Playhouse passed into the hands of the Shuberts, who planned to make the theatre more attractive to audiences by eliminating the second balcony. The crowds packing the Playhouse for the premiere run of Tennessee Williams's *The Glass Managerie* thought the theatre was just fine as it was, and the scheme was dropped. Following a brief stint as an ABC Radio studio from 1949–1952, the Shuberts streamlined the auditorium somewhat by removing the boxes and increasing the capacity to 994. Despite this attention, seven years passed before Anne Bancroft and Patty Duke opened in the theatre's next smash hit, *The Miracle Worker*. In 1963 the comedy *Never Too Late* began a two-and-a-half year run, eventually claiming the house record of one thousand performances. During the run of *Never Too Late* the Shuberts sold the Playhouse to a group of developers who planned to build an office tower on the site. The Playhouse closed permanently following the long-run comedy *The Impossible Years* in 1968, but before demolition began there was one last booking. Under the direction of Mel Brooks film crews moved in to shoot the classic comedy *The Producers*. Both the interior and exterior of the theatre can be seen during the "Springtime For Hitler" sequences. Today, the site of the Playhouse is occupied by the McGraw-Hill Building.

FOLIES-BERGERE

210 West 46th Street Herts & Tallant, 1911

It was not too common for new theatres to be described as "ingenious" or "odd," but that's exactly how some critics saw the new Folies-Bergere in 1911. Proprietors Henry B. Harris and Jesse L. Lasky combined the best elements of the Folies-Bergere in Paris and the old Koster and Bial's Music Hall in New York to create a unique place of entertainment—the district's first theatre-restaurant. From Broadway the Folies-Bergere was impossible to miss. Huge metal signs shaped like banners spelled out the music hall's name in electric lights. Below the bronze cornice a mural depicted all the characters of vaudeville marching to the throne of "Les Folies-Bergere." This colorful relief was surrounded by the theatre's glazed terra-cotta facade. The turquoise blue, old ivory, and gold of the Venetian-style tiles made the Folies-Bergere the brightest, most eye-catching theatre along the Rialto. Three entrances studded with glass mosaics and framed in carved oak led to a stone and white marble lobby containing the box office, cloak rooms, and elevator to the two balconies. The auditorium was small and shallow, with room for about eight hundred persons. Most contemporary accounts of the house note the softness of the decorations, an effect achieved by the rose, pearl gray, and gold color scheme. The orchestra seating was arranged on rows of terraces around tables of various sizes, each illuminated by pink-shaded candelabra. Both balconies had regular theatre seats, but the lower tier's first row was devoted to private tables separated by iron grills. The space reserved for proscenium boxes, which were absent at the Folies-Bergere, was decorated by ornamental plasterwork. The arch itself was also ornate and crowned by two trumpeting angels. In the basement were lounges and dressing rooms for patrons, a barber shop, manicurists, and valets. Beneath the stage, carved from the solid bedrock, was a large gourmet kitchen. The opening of the Folies-Bergere on 27 April 1911 was a grand event. Diners arrived at six for appetizers and a vaudeville show. As main courses were served the entertainment progressed to a "profane burlesque" called *Hell,* and a "satirical revuette" entitled *Gaby.* The evening ended at 1:30 A.M. after supper and a two-hour cabaret. Although critics were impressed, the theatre's premiere was not perfect. Between the acts of *Hell* a standpipe in the elevator shaft burst, drenching the lobby and rear orchestra. It seemed, however, to be of little consequence to the majority of the audience. They went home happy, a little soggy, and considerably poorer, for it was estimated the evening cost each couple over $35. Despite the glowing reviews, Harris and Lasky's Folies-Bergere proved to be simply too expensive in an era of fifty-cent theatre tickets and dollar meals. After three months the house closed for major remodeling. When it reopened as the Fulton in October, the tables and kitchen were gone. It had become just another Broadway playhouse, albeit a pretty one. *The Cave Man* christened the Fulton, but it fared considerably worse than *Hell* had, lasting only two weeks. Although it would be two years before the house had a true hit, there were two noteworthy produc-

ABOVE : Interior view of Broadway's first theatre-restaurant in 1911. (TH)

ABOVE : The Folies-Bergere, 1911. (TH)

OPPOSITE PAGE : Exterior view, 1974. (NvH)

tions in 1912: *The Yellow Jacket,* a comedy, and *Damaged Goods,* a frank drama about venereal disease. Success came to the Fulton in 1913 in the guise of *The Misleading Lady,* a comedy featuring Lewis Stone and, in his Broadway debut, George Abbott. After its 183 performances, the farce *Twin Beds* played 411 times. The Fulton's numerous bookings during the next decade included the 1922 premiere of *Abie's Irish Rose* (which moved to the Republic for the majority of its record-breaking eight years on Broadway). Few of the Fulton's shows ran longer than ten weeks, though, leaving the house dark for months at a time. The Fulton's luck changed in 1925 with the booking of Sam Jaffe and George Jessel in *The Jazz Singer,* a 303-performance hit. Beatrice Lillie and Helen Broderick appeared in Vincent Youmans' musical *Oh, Please,* followed in 1927 by Bela Lugosi in *Dracula.* The next few years saw appearances by George M. Cohan, Dorothy Gish, Maurice Chevalier, and Duke Ellington and his Cotton Club Orchestra. With the exception of the occasional movie or burlesque show, the Fulton made it through the depression still devoted to the live theatre. The next hit, *New Faces of 1934,* was the first in a series of successful revues introducing fresh talent. Imogene Coca and Henry Fonda were welcomed to Broadway in this edition. In 1940 the house flirted briefly with radio, but returned to legitimate theatre in 1941 with a smash. *Arsenic and Old Lace* played most of its 1,444 performances at the playhouse on 46th Street. The 1950s brought Audrey Hepburn in *Gigi,* the hit comedy *The Seven-Year Itch,* and a new name to the Fulton. On 21 November 1955 the charming showplace was renamed the Helen Hayes Theatre in honor of the actress' fifty years on stage. "This," Miss Hayes remarked at the time, "is my finest hour." For the next twenty-five years the Helen Hayes continued to be one of the district's more popular theatres. *Long Day's Journey Into Night* won a posthumous Pulitzer Prize for Eugene O'Neill in 1956 and Jean Kerr's 1961 comedy *Mary, Mary* won the long-run title with 1,572 performances. The seventies saw successful runs of *Hadrian VII*, *The Me Nobody Knows*, and *The Royal Family* at the Hayes. During this period the most important drama in the theatre's history was being played out in the offices of real estate developers, landmarks commissioners, and even the White House. In 1973

BELOW : Proscenium, 1911. (TH)

ABOVE : Interior, 1973. (NvH)

John Portman proposed to improve the neighborhood by building a luxury hotel on the sites then occupied by the Astor, Victoria, Bijou, Morosco, and Helen Hayes theatres. For nine years preservation groups battled to save the five historic theatres, taking their fight as far as the U.S. Federal Court, where it was argued that members of the Reagan administration pressured the Advisory Council on Historic Preservation to approve the demolition and deny petitions to consider alternate plans that would save at least some of the buildings. The Federal Court issued an injunction while it considered the question of undue political influence, but the order applied only to the Hayes. As its fate was being decided the four other theatres were reduced to rubble. Finally, in 1982 the court ruled in favor of Portman. After three weeks and $200,000 was spent to salvage architecturally significant parts of the theatre, the Helen Hayes was demolished. The loss of the five buildings robbed the city of 347 combined years of theatre history. There was one positive result, however. In response to the outcry from theatre professionals, the press, and the public, preservation groups have successfully obtained landmark status for nearly all of Times Square's remaining legitimate theatres.

BELOW : Interior, 1973. (NvH)

BELOW : Demolition, 1982. (LS)

48TH STREET THEATRE

157 West 48th Street   William A. Swasey, 1912

After establishing the Playhouse on 48th Street, producer William A. Brady put up a second theatre practically next door. Although the 48th Street Theatre was an elegant addition to the roster of Broadway playhouses, it would be years before it matched the smash successes of some of its neighbors. Built on the site of an old apartment house in 1912, the 48th Street was quite similar to other theatres of the times. Behind a small lobby were a fourteen-row fan-shaped orchestra section, eight boxes, and two balconies, for a total seating capacity of 969. The wall hangings and upholstery were light gray, the proscenium and plaster decorations silver and ivory. The stage was of average size (32 feet deep with a 31-foot wide proscenium opening), with the room off stage left restricted due to an unusually angled back wall. Perhaps the most striking feature of the 48th Street was its facade. Colonial in design, glazed white terra-cotta trimmings on a limestone base provided relief from the red-brick exterior. Below the peaked cornice seven multi-paned windows faced the street. The overall appearance, which was similar to the Belasco Theatre on 44th Street, was considered by many to be quite pleasing. The 48th Street Theatre opened its doors on 11 August 1912 with *Just Like John,* a comedy Brady co-produced with playwright George Broadhurst (who built his own theatre in partnership with the Shuberts five years later.) *Just Like John* was not a success; nor was the theatre's second play. But the third and fourth shows, *Never Say Die* and *Today,* were popular and collectively played over 400 times. In 1915 *The Thirteenth Chair*'s ten-month run held the record at the 48th Street until *The Squall* played the first of its 444 performances in 1926.

During the intervening ten years, the 48th Street played host to a number of plays, some of which proved popular, and most of which are long forgotten. Remembered from the many casts, though, are Otto Krueger, Katharine Cornell, Mischa Auer, and Spring Byington. In 1922 the actor's union leased the playhouse as a home for their Equity Players. Equity's lack of success suggested that the union should refrain from hiring actors and just stick to representing them, which is exactly what the union did by 1925.

A number of minor hits followed *The Squall,* beginning with *Cock Robin,* a comic mystery by Philip Barry and Elmer Rice, in 1928. *Brothers, Unexpected Husband,* and *The Streets of New York* followed with modest runs. In 1935 Montgomery Clift and Thomas Mitchell chalked up 204 performances in *Fly Away Home,* a drama which was succeeded by a series of failures. In 1937 four of the boxes were removed as the house was renovated as a first-run movie theatre. The name was changed to the Windsor, but the film policy held for only a brief time. By November the Windsor's stage was back in use with *Work is for Horses,* and in January one of the decade's most important works opened there. *The Cradle Will Rock* addressed the struggle between labor and management during the troubled economic times of the thirties. Mark Blitzstein's opera starring Will Geer and Howard da Silva played 108 times.

ABOVE : 1955 demolition of the theatre following the collapse of the water tank on its roof. (LC)

The theatre did no better in booking a runaway smash hit as the Windsor than it had as the 48th Street. In 1943, wanting to avoid possible confusion with the Windor Theatre in the Bronx, which played popularly-priced legit, the house returned to its original name. The following year it found that magic show. Mary Chase's charming play about Elwood P. Dowd and a six-foot tall rabbit named *Harvey* entertained audiences for over four years and 1,775 performances. The theatre's last hit, *Stalag 17,* was playing the first of its 472 performances in May 1951. Flops followed, including Robert Preston in *Men of Distinction* and a curious "Hillbilly Folk Musical" called *Hayride.* In April 1955 the long-running *Tea and Sympathy* moved in to play its final ten weeks, and by June the theatre was dark, waiting for the fall's new crop of shows. Nine weeks later disaster struck. At 9:00 A.M. on 24 August, the steel beams supporting a water tank above the 48th Street Theatre's roof finally gave way to years of corrosion. The full tank, which supplied the playhouse's sprinkler system with 10,000 gallons of water, tore a 500 square foot hole in the roof as it crashed into the theatre below. The orchestra pit, seven rows of seats, and two boxes were demolished. In a top-floor apartment next door to the theatre Mrs. Anna Berman and her 10-year-old son Arthur were seated on a bed, enjoying a mild summer breeze drifting through an open window. They were drenched, and presumably quite surprised, by the thousands of gallons of water which followed. Fortunately, no one was seriously injured by the accident. The owners of the theatre planned to restore the house only if it could be enlarged at the same time. When studies of the site made it clear that there was insufficient room to expand, the 48th Street Theatre's demolition was completed by more familiar means. Today the site is a parking garage.

ABOVE : Interior, circa 1920. (MCNY)

ELTINGE 42ND STREET THEATRE

236 West 42nd Street Thomas W. Lamb, 1912

There are theatres in New York City named after actors and actresses, playwrights and producers, even streets and buildings. But only one playhouse, in a metropolis with hundreds of them, was ever named in honor of a female impersonator. Julian Eltinge was the early twentieth century's most popular male interpreter of female roles. His manager and producer, Al Woods, built Eltinge an intimate playhouse to reward his nation-wide success. It was the eighth theatre built on 42nd Street and as unique in appearance as the performer after whom it was named. Architect Thomas A. Lamb, who would later be known for his sumptuous movie palaces, designed an exterior for the Eltinge that at once was bold and delicate. The main feature was a large multi-paned window described by a broad carved-stone arch. The light-colored facade was decorated by terra-cotta ornaments tinted in green, blue, orange, and red. A glass and steel marquee, tiled roof, and quartet of electric display signs completed the street exterior. The auditorium, which was reached by way of a tiny lobby, accommodated 900 persons in the orchestra, two balconies, and eight boxes. According to *The New York Times,* the Eltinge offered patrons sitting downstairs an unusual choice. "Instead of being of uniform size, as is the prevailing custom, the orchestra chairs will be of three different sizes, so that slender, medium, and stout patrons may request seats most conducive to their personal comfort. For the obese theatre lovers this will be a genuine treat." The color of the auditorium was quite light, with gold being the predominant highlighting tone. The side walls curved up to a ceiling light six feet in diameter. Classical Egyptian motifs decorated the graceful proscenium arch, while the large mural above it depicted Roman and Greek figures. The overlapping periods confused some critics. "What the designer intended when he decorated the boxes with bacchantic figures wearing Egyptian headresses and playing pipes," wrote the *Times,* "can only be imagined." The Eltinge 42nd Street Theatre opened on 11 September 1912 with a tremendous success. The premiere production, *Within the Law,* ran an astonishing 541 times and established a house record that was never broken. More hits followed. *The Song of Songs* began a six-month run in 1914, followed by *Fair and Warmer,* a 1915 farce that enjoyed almost a year of performances. *Up in Mabel's Room, The Girl in the Limousine,* and *Ladies Night* also had extended runs during the theatre's first decade. Although forgotten today, these popular farces established the Eltinge as a prime house for comedy. Heavier melodramas had their place, too, but often with less success. While Somerset Maugham's *East of Suez* managed 100 performances in 1921, *Murder on the Second Floor* played only 45 times in 1929 despite having Laurence Olivier as its star. *Love, Honor, and Betray* featured Alice Brady and Clark Gable in 1930, but it also was in residence at the Eltinge only briefly. The succeeding production, *First Night,* proved to be the theatre's final dramatic attraction. When it closed after 88 performances in 1931 the Eltinge abandoned the legitimate stage. It did not, however, give up live shows.

LEFT : Eltinge Theatre, named after popular female impersonator Julian Eltinge, in 1912. (MCNY)

ABOVE : Eltinge theatre, interior, 1912. (MCNY)

Along with the Republic Theatre down the street, the Eltinge switched to drama of another kind—the bump and grind. For over ten years strippers teased their audiences and comics told off-color jokes from the stage of the Eltinge. In 1942, after Mayor LaGuardia finally told the strippers to stop taking it off, the house returned to the comedies it knew so well from the glory days of 42nd Street.

Only this time the medium was different. The theatre reopened in the summer of 1942 as the Laff Movie, a film house dedicated to unspooling the latest Hollywood comedy. By the end of 1954 the theatre was called the Empire, grinding out second-run films around the clock. That policy continued until the theatre closed its doors in the mid-1980s.

The Empire will play an unusual part in the new 42nd Street. Both the interior and exterior have been landmarked by the city and will be restored as the grand entrance lobby of a twenty-five screen movie complex to be built by the AMC theatre chain (renderings of the proposed renovation appear on page 266). In order to create space for the cinemas, AMC plans—in late 1997—to lift the 4-million-pound Empire off its foundation and move it 200 feet down the block.

LEFT : Eltinge interior, 1989. (MH)

BELOW : In 1954 the house was renamed the Empire; thirty-five years later it stands closed. (MH)

ELTINGE 42ND STREET THEATRE

ABOVE : The auditorium chandelier was six feet in diameter. (AB)

LEFT : Ceiling detail, 1989. (MH)

BELOW : Interior view, 1989. (MH)

ABOVE : Weber and Fields' Music Hall, 1912. The large windows on the top floor opened to allow breezes to cool the roof garden. (AB)

WEBER & FIELDS' MUSIC HALL

216 West 44th Street William A. Swasey, 1913

Shortly after Lee and J.J. Shubert's 1912 announcement that their latest theatre would be called the Palace Music Hall, rival Martin Beck revealed that his new vaudeville house would also be called the Palace. Never ones to be sentimental about theatre names, the Shuberts instead chose to honor the comedy team of Weber and Fields, which had reunited after years of feuding. In a single step the Shuberts out-maneuvered their competition and established a relationship with one of the era's top box office draws. The Shuberts built Weber & Fields' Music Hall directly behind the New York Times' 43rd Street annex, on a site owned by Vincent Astor. Although the music hall shared an arcade with the newspaper, the main entrance for audiences, actors, and patrons of the roof garden and basement rathskeller was on 44th Street. The ornate cornices and capitals of the brick facade gave the building a classical appearance, but the overall effect was diminished by the bulky enclosure of the roof theatre. Inside, though, the lines and proportions remained clean and graceful. Two shallow balconies were set back and staggered, allowing for the auditorium's spacious, open feeling. A chandelier hung from each panel of the ceiling; the total number of auditorium chandeliers (16) must have been some sort of record. Of the 1,463 seats, one thousand were on the orchestra level. Two tiers of boxes brought the focus towards the square proscenium. The most unique feature of the house was the location of its dressing rooms. The unusual length of the theatre's plot enabled them to be placed behind the stage rather than off one of the wings. The long, narrow corridor had space for five stage-level dressing rooms. Weber & Fields' parodies of current Broadway hits had always been popular, so it made sense to open the new theatre with a proven formula. A double-bill of *Roly-Poly* and *Without the Law* greeted first-nighters on 21 November 1912. Despite a warm welcome from critics and audiences, the comedians ended the run after less than two months when they split for a final time. Weber and Fields never again appeared together on a New York stage. The Shuberts, realizing there no longer was a "Weber & Fields," hastily changed the theatre's name to the 44th Street with the booking of *The Geisha* in March 1913. That October, Lew Fields returned to his former namesake as the producer of the vaudeville *A Glimpse of the Great White Way,* a one-week flop. In the years that followed, the Shuberts booked operettas, English musicals, classical repertory, and extravaganzas by Rudolf Friml and Sigmund Romberg. In 1915 Friml wrote the music for the 44th Street's first real hit; during its seven-month run Arthur Hammerstein's production of *Katrinka* set a new standard for Broadway operettas. Later Al Jolson starred in *Big Boy,* followed by *Song of the Flame,* a musical co-authored by George Gershwin. The next hits were a revue, *A Night in Spain,* and *The Five O'Clock Girl,* a musical. Without question the decade's zaniest hit came from the Marx Brothers in 1928. The antics of Groucho, Harpo, Chico, and Zeppo in *Animal Crackers* kept audiences howling for six months. Fanny Brice, Bob Hope, Walter Hampden, Lee J. Cobb, Elia Kazan, Burgess Meredith, and Ingrid Bergman

151

ABOVE : Above Weber and Fields' was another theatre, known first as Lew Fields' 44th Street Roof Garden and later as the Nora Bayes. It operated as a fully equipped Broadway house through the thirties. (AB)

appeared in a variety of productions in the thirties and into the forties. The most memorable of these was Gertrude Stein's 1934 opera *Four Saints in Three Acts*. From its nearly incomprehensible libretto to its unusual cellophane sets, the show made no compromises for the average audience. Although the opera was much talked about it was much avoided, and soon the 44th Street was available for more accessible works. The last of these, 1942's *Rosalinda,* set the house record. The adaptation of *Die Fledermaus* ran 521 performances.

While the main stage was presenting musicals and dramas, both the roof theatre and basement cafe enjoyed varying degrees of success. The upstairs auditorium began life in June 1913 as Lew Fields' 44th Street Roof Garden. After vacating the downstairs house, Fields produced and starred in the roof theatre's premiere production, *All Aboard.* It was one of the theatre's few hits. The house changed

ABOVE : Weber and Fields' Music Hall Boxes, 1912. (TH)

ABOVE : Weber and Fields' Music Hall, 1912. (TH)

names nine times in twenty-four years, but was best known as the Nora Bayes Theatre (named in honor of the popular musical actress). High points in its history include Victor Herbert's *My Golden Girl,* George Gershwin's *Our Nell,* Little Theatre tournaments, Pat O'Brien in *Gertie,* and Irving Caesar's *The Wonder Bar,* starring Al Jolson and Arthur Treacher. In the late thirties the Nora Bayes housed productions of the Federal Theatre Project, amateur theatre groups, marionette companies, and dance troupes. By the forties the house was mostly dark. In comparison, the basement cafe had two great bursts of popularity. During prohibition it was a favorite meeting place for conversation (and perhaps a bootleg drink or two) known as the Little Club. Twenty years later it became famous once again, this time as the Stage Door Canteen. Here soldiers could relax while on leave, shoot some pool, or swing with a visiting star. In 1943 the New York Times took possession of the structure for use as a warehouse for huge rolls of newsprint. The following year the Times filed plans to raze the theatre and replace it with an 11-story structure to include additional printing presses. The 44th Street Theatre came down in 1945; the Times building constructed on the site still stands today.

PRINCESS THEATRE

104 WEST 39TH STREET   WILLIAM A. SWASEY, 1913

On a narrow site on 39th Street just west of Sixth Avenue, producer F. Ray Comstock, actor-director Holbrook Blinn, and the Shuberts built a small theatre planned especially for the production of intimate short plays. But during its checkered career the Princess, which was one of Broadway's smallest houses, became best known instead for a remarkable series of shows that set the standard for early musical comedies. From the street the Princess was quite ordinary; only a large electric sign gave any hint to the diversions offered inside. The auditorium, however, was quite ornate. While most of the 299 seats were on the orchestra floor, architect W. A. Swasey placed some in the boxes that flanked the curved proscenium and gave the Princess an elegance not found in other theatres of its size. The auditorium walls were decorated with ornamental plasterwork and exquisite French tapestries. The French influenced more than the theatre's decor. The Grand Guignol in Paris had enjoyed many profitable seasons presenting bills of one-act plays. It was the success of this policy that Messrs. Comstock, Blinn, and Shubert hoped to duplicate on Broadway. Unfortunately, it lost something in the translation. The Princess Players, under the direction of Blinn, opened the theatre on 14 March 1913 with a bill of five plays—*The Switchboard, Fear, Fancy Free, Any Night,* and *A Tragedy of the Future.* The shows closed when hot weather arrived 115 performances later. The Players launched a second series of one-acters in September, but after their third season it was apparent that the theatre's debt would be better served by a change in policy. Comstock decided to go with musical comedy, provided the sets, costume changes, and cast size were kept to a minimum. Jerome Kern and Guy Bolton were hired to write *Nobody Home,* which Comstock produced in 1915 for only $7,500. The show lasted five months, enough to encourage Comstock to commission a second musical, *Very Good Eddie.* This time the songs and jokes were based on characters and their situations, which was not the standard practice in musical comedies. *Very Good Eddie*'s 341 performances made it clear that audiences approved of Kern and Bolton's new form. The third Princess musical, *Go To It,* lacked their participation and was a quick flop in 1916. The following year Kern and Bolton returned for the theatre's fourth tuner, and it was a smash. P.G. Wodehouse joined the creative team for *Oh, Boy!,* the most successful of the Princess musicals. Rave reviews kept *Oh, Boy!* open for 463 showings and confirmed that a new type of entertainment had developed at the Princess Theatre. *Oh Lady! Lady!* in 1918 was Kern's final Princess musical, and the series ended following the modest success of *Oh, My Dear!* in 1919. The Princess Theatre musicals proved to be a hard act to follow, although *Six Characters in Search of an Author* managed a 17-week stay in 1921. George Abbott appeared in the short-lived *White Desert,* a 1922 drama which was Maxwell Anderson's first Broadway production. More failures followed, and the Princess received very little notice at all

LEFT : Princess interior, 1913. (TM)

until police condemned its 1927 play *The Virgin Man* as immoral. The notoriety didn't help, however, and it also failed.   he house was renamed for actress Lucille La Verne when she starred in *Sun-Up* in 1928, but the following spring it was once again known as the Princess. The New York Theatre Assembly took it over in the fall of 1929 and christened it the Assembly, but their residence lasted only four months. In the early thirties the Princess was showing films as the Reo Cinema, and its career as a legitimate theatre appeared to be most definitely over a few years later when the International Ladies Garment Worker's Union acquired it as a recreation center. But the theatre is full of surprises, as evidenced by the unexpected success of the union-sponsored revue that reopened the Princess (now called the Labor Stage) in 1937. *Pins and Needles* went on to become the longest-running musical of the day, dividing its 1,108 performances between the Labor Stage and larger Windsor Theatre on 48th Street.   hen *Pins and Needles* moved uptown, the union reclaimed the Princess as its recreation hall. In 1944 a theatre workshop was held there, and in 1947 the building reopened to the general public as a foreign film theatre, Cinema Dante. In 1948 the name was changed to Little Met (lest anyone confuse it with the big Metropolitan Opera House down the block), and in 1952 to Cinema Verdi.

Standing on the edge of the theatre district, its size and location made the old Princess obsolete. The playhouse gave way to the wrecker's ball in June 1955.

CANDLER THEATRE

226 WEST 42ND STREET   THOMAS W. LAMB, 1914

The Candler Theatre was the fifth major playhouse to open on 42nd Street's south side. Like the New Amsterdam and Liberty theatres that flanked it, the Candler's narrow lobby extended through the block to the main auditorium on 41st Street. While this configuration may have enabled stores and offices, as well as the theatres, to have a desirable entrance on the main thoroughfare, it also turned the north side of 41st Street into one giant brick wall supporting a tangled mass of iron fire escapes. The gloom the Candler added to 41st Street, however, was more than justified by the glamour it brought to 42nd Street. The glittering marquee that announced the theatre's presence was mounted on the front of the Candler Building, a five-story office structure built with proceeds from the Candler family's Coca-Cola fortune. The riches of the new playhouse, evident immediately upon entering the 25-foot wide lobby, caused one correspondent from the *Dramatic News* to glowingly describe the Candler, with the help of the theatre's press agent, shortly after it opened:

> Entering from the street, one passes through a marble vestibule, the ceiling of which is beautifully stenciled in gold. This leads to a foyer, and from here you pass into a tapestry hall, the walls of which are covered with six loom tapestries by Albert Herter depicting different Shakesperean scenes. The two larger ones represent scenes from *The Merchant of Venice* and *Othello*. The smaller ones are from the comedies. The lobby is exquisitely ornamented with flower panels characteristic of the 18th century school. The whole is carried out in Caen stone and conveys an air of dignity and purity. The passageways and staircases are of a magnitude that shows no attempt at economizing in space.
>
> The auditorium of the Candler, while comparatively small—or, to use the more fitting term, intimate—makes an impression of vastness quite beyond its actual dimensions. The reason of this is its perfection in design and the beauty of its lines and curves. The house is one of the handsomest and most magnificently appointed theatres in New York. The first floor contains 625 seats, while the one balcony, of the cantilever type, seats 575. The architecture is Italian Renaissance; the prevailing tone is mouse color and orange. Carpets and seats are in harmonious keeping with the general scheme, the latter with tapestry backs of twelve different designs, giving an unusual effect to the lower floor. Generous promenades are provided here as well as on the balcony. A feature which cannot fail to create general interest is the very beautiful mural panel which covers the wall of the lower promenade. The subject is a "Fete Champetre," painted in oil by Herter. It is, in the truest sense of the word, a work of art which leaves a most pleasing impression. ""

The lessees and owners of the Candler were George M. Cohan and Sam H. Harris, a Mr. Sol Bloom, and George Kleine, a producer of "photo-dramatic marvels," or movies. Although Cohan and Harris would soon turn the house over to legit, the opening attraction on 7 May 1914 was a film from Kleine, *Anthony and Cleopatra*. Cohan and Harris'

LEFT : Candler Theatre, 1934. Producer Sam H. Harris
renamed it in 1921. (LC)

turn came three months later with Elmer Rice's *On Trial.* The Candler's first stage presentation was a long-run hit, as were the two shows that followed. In September 1916 the theatre was renamed the Cohan and Harris after the successful producing partners.

Between 1917 and 1920 *A Tailor Made Man, Three Faces East,* and *Welcome Stranger* each gave more than 300 performances. The team of Cohan and Harris had made

ABOVE : Candler interior, 1914. (TH)

their theatre one of 42nd Street's favorites, but in 1921 they split. Cohan went on to pursue other opportunities while his former partner took over the playhouse, which was rechristened the Sam H. Harris. A year later the Harris entered the history books with

Arthur Hopkins' record-breaking production of *Hamlet*. John Barrymore appeared in the title role 101 consecutive times, beating out Edwin Booth's record by a single performance. The decade that followed brought many popular shows to the Harris. George Abbott's *Love 'Em and Leave 'Em*; Paul Muni in *We Americans*; *Mendel, Inc.* with comedy stars Joe Smith and Charles Dale; Spencer Tracy in *The Last Mile*; and *Rhapsody in Black* staring Ethel Waters each enjoyed long runs on the street of hits. In 1933 George M. Cohan returned to his old stomping ground in *Pigeons and People*, a comedy that only managed a modest two-month stay. When it closed, the Harris joined many of the neighboring theatres by abandoning live theatre in favor of films. The Harris remained a movie theatre for fifty-five years until it was closed in anticipation of 42nd Street's renewal. But with only the preservation of its 41st Street facade required under the redevelopment guidelines, the theatre will most likely be gutted and rebuilt when it becomes a part of the first American home of Madame Tussaud's Wax Museum, in 1998.

TOP LEFT : Candler Theatre balcony exit, 1989. (MH)
BOTTOM LEFT : Exterior view, 1989. (MH)
BELOW : Candler interior, 1989. (MH)

ABOVE : Charles Hopkins' Punch and Judy Theatre, 1914. (LC)

PUNCH & JUDY THEATRE

153 WEST 49TH STREET MURRAY & DANA, 1914

As mammoth theatres like the Hippodrome, American, and Century competed for patrons with giant stage extravaganzas or elaborate vaudeville, some insightful managers thought there might be a need for playhouses more suited for intimate comedies and dramas. Winthrop Ames built the Little Theatre in 1912, F. Ray Comstock opened the Princess a year later, and in 1914 actor-producer Charles Hopkins premiered his tiny gem, the Punch & Judy. Tucked away on 49th Street east of Seventh Avenue, the Punch & Judy was called "New York's cutest playhouse." While that may have been open to some debate, the theatre probably qualified as the city's most unique. The forty-foot wide exterior of the theatre was finished in buff plaster accented with brown woodwork. The theatre's name, along with orange and blue paintings of the battling Punch and Judy puppets, decorated the three-story facade.

Past the tiny lobby, ushers dressed in Elizabethan costumes greeted ticketholders in an auditorium that resembled the courtyard of an old English inn. The eighteen rows of seats were actually comfortable wooden benches upholstered in dark leather. Mezzanine boxes seating between two and six persons each surrounded the auditorium on three sides. They were decorated with Louis XIII-style tapestries in dark greens, reds, and blues and lit by electric lamps in old English candle fixtures. The period effect was completed by a high, flat ceiling supported by heavy wooden beams. Although the Punch & Judy could accommodate an audience of only 299 at any given performance, it boasted a standard-sized stage thirty-one feet deep and almost forty feet wide. Hopkins starred in the theatre's first production, *The Marriage of Colombine.* It was not a success. Subsequent shows, comedies with titles like *Where's Your Wife?* and *Merchants of Venus* did not fare well either. In fact, for its first ten years the Punch and Judy managed to house only two modest hits. The more successful of the pair, *Rollo's Wild Oats,* a comedy starring Roland Young, managed a seven-month run in 1920. By the mid-twenties, after a particularly bad slump, the theatre had the dubious distinction of having booked eleven straight flops.

Something had to be done, so in 1926 Hopkins renamed the playhouse after himself. For little apparent reason the theatre then started to enjoy some successes, most of which have been long forgotten—*Devil in the Cheese* starring Bela Lugosi and Frederic March, Henry Hull in the ten-month run of *The Ivory Door,* and the theatre's longest running tenant, *Mrs. Moonlight,* which kept audiences laughing for 321 performances in 1930.

Three years later, as Broadway felt the devastating effects of the depression, the tiny Charles Hopkins was no longer viable as a legitimate theatre. Retaining a financial interest in it, Hopkins leased his playhouse to movie exhibitors. In 1934, the name was changed to the Westminster Cinema and the programs were restricted to British-made films. A year later it was called the World Theatre, and the films became French and Italian. Ultimately, the World presented both foreign films and second-runs of the Hollywood variety, and remained a movie theatre for decades.

ABOVE : Punch and Judy interior, 1914. (LC)

By the sixties the theatre district was in decline. Many movie houses, the World among them, survived by screening softcore porno films. Shows at the World became triple-X with the 1972 premiere of *Deep Throat,* perhaps the most famous, or infamous, tenant in the entire history of the theatre. In 1982, after it became known that Manhattan's most notorious porno house was owned by the respectable Rockefeller Group, blue movies got the boot. Embassy Theatres took over the operation of the house, renamed it the Embassy 49th Street, and returned it to instant respectability with its first booking, a Walt Disney movie. Over the years and changes of name and policy, Charles Hopkins' little theatre retained its intimacy, looks, and even its stage, dressing rooms, and ring of boxes. In 1987, however, it lost the final battle against rising land values and was razed. The site, currently vacant, is due to be part of another skyscraper.

ABOVE : As the World Theatre in 1975. (NvH)

MOROSCO THEATRE

217 WEST 45TH STREET   HERBERT J. KRAPP, 1917

Although West Coast producer Oliver Morosco managed six successful legitimate houses in Los Angeles, he often found it difficult to secure suitable New York theatres for his plays. The Shubert brothers, wanting a partner for their next construction project, approached Morosco with a plan to develop a plot they owned across from the Astor Hotel. The playhouse born from this collaboration became one of the most desireable and successful theatres on Broadway. The Morosco was not an ornate or particularly unique theatre. A metal parapet crowned the simple brick and terra cotta facade. Under an iron and glass canopy three pairs of doors led to a small marble lobby illuminated by lights concealed in an antique bronze cornice. The lobby's doors and furnishings were finished in matching bronze, while the cove ceiling was treated in dull gold. Inside the auditorium the walls were painted a warm gray, the side panels relieved by mural decorations set in oval pendants, and the carpets and curtains tinted in shades of violet. The rich glow from four crystal chandeliers added to the tasteful, if subdued, interior design. The theatre's 954 seats were divided among the orchestra, single balcony, and 14 boxes. (The eight orchestra boxes were later replaced by regular seats, a move that increased the capacity by 55). During its long life the Morosco had its fair share of flops, but its many successes made the house one of Broadway's most popular. Although considered ideal for plays, the Morosco actually opened with one of its few musicals. *Canary Cottage,* with a score by future theatre manager Earl Carroll, began its 112-performance run on 5 February 1917. Eugene O'Neill's first full-length Broadway drama, *Beyond the Horizon,* opened at the Morosco in 1920 and won the Pulitzer Prize. Later that year the mystery *The Bat* thrilled the first of its 867 audiences. The 1925 Pulitzer went to *Craig's Wife,* which was followed (after seven flops) by Katharine Cornell's star turn in Somerset Maugham's *The Letter.* Other names appearing on the marquee in subsequent years included Katharine Hepburn, Lillian Gish, Ruth Gordon, and Tallullah Bankhead. In 1943 *Sons and Soldiers,* starring Gregory Peck, Karl Malden, and Stella Adler, only lasted three weeks. Shows that followed were considerably more successful, however. The comedy *The Voice of the Turtle* closed in 1947 after setting the house record of 1,310 performances. In 1949 Arthur Miller's *Death of a Salesman* premiered at the Morosco and became a modern classic during its 742 showings. The acclaim given to Tennessee William's *Cat On A Hot Tin Roof* in 1955 served to reinforce the Morosco's place as a home for the best drama on Broadway. Over the next twenty-five years the Morosco lived up to its reputation. Richard Burton and Helen Hayes in *Time Remembered,* Henry Fonda in *Silent Night, Lonely Night,* Melvyn Douglas in *The Best Man,* Woody Allen's *Don't Drink the Water,* Julie Harris in the comedy *Forty Carats,* and John Gielgud and Ralph Richardson in *Home* were some of the hits that carried the Morosco into the Seventies. In 1973 a revival of *A Moon for the Misbegotten,* starring Jason Robards and Colleen Dewhurst,

ABOVE : Morosco interior, 1917. Despite plans to enlarge its lobby, the Morosco changed very little during its 65-year history. (AB)

more than quadrupled the run of the original production. *The Shadow Box* won a Pulitzer in 1977, and the following year *Da* achieved the longest run of the decade—nearly 700 performances. *Da* was also the Morosco's final success. After the single performance of the 1981 comedy *I Won't Dance*, the theatre was closed while the courts decided its fate. Developers hoped to raze it along with the Astor, Victoria, Bijou, and Helen Hayes theatres in order to put up a high-rise hotel in its place. Preservationists, performers, and producers fought to save the Hayes and Morosco. But with the support of the city, state, and ultimately, the White House, the developers were granted the right to clear the site. With its seats still in place the Morosco was hastily demolished in March 1982.

LEFT : The Morosco in 1973. Additional views of the theatre appear in the following chapter on the Bijou. (NvH)

LEFT : Interior, 1973. (NvH)

ABOVE AND BELOW : Demolition, 1982. (LS)

BIJOU THEATRE

With only 603 seats, the Bijou was the smallest theatre built by the Shuberts. The brick, stone, and terra-cotta facade matched that of the Shubert's adjacent Morosco Theatre, which was designed in tandem with the Bijou by Shubert house architect Herbert J. Krapp. Beyond a small lobby was a blue, ivory, and gold auditorium decorated in the style of Louis XVI. (This was a logical design choice as the Bijou was originally conceived as the Theatre Francais, a home for local French theatre.) The audience at the 12 April 1917 opening of the Bijou saw *The Knife,* a thriller. It proved less than successful, running only eleven weeks. For two years J.J. Shubert was unable to find a hit for his small playhouse, but in October 1919 that changed when *His Honor, Abe Potash* moved in for a 215-performance stay. More hits followed, including the 1926 revival of *What Every Woman Knows,* starring Helen Hayes. After two years of flops the comedy *Skidding,* with Walter Abel and Clara Blandick, took up residence for 448 performances. The Bijou's first (and last) long run of the thirties opened in December 1931. *Springtime for Henry* satisfied fans of farce for more than six months. Despite displaying the talents of Flora Robson, Shirley Booth, and Dorothy Parker over the next four years, nothing at the Bijou worked, including a stint as New York's only all-cartoon movie theatre in 1935. After *The Sap Runs High* flopped in 1936, the movie screen went back in until the following year, when the theatre closed. The Bijou remained dark well into 1943, when it was relit for legitimate producers. While the neighboring theatres on 45th Street presented one hit after another, the Bijou's only notable tenant during this period was *Life With Father,* moved over from the Empire at the end of its record-breaking run. Movies returned to the Bijou from 1947 to 1953, followed by another six years as a legitimate venue. This time the Bijou achieved some popularity housing revues starring Libby Holman, Ruth Draper, Joyce Grenfell, Anthony Newley, and Mort Sahl. Plays were also presented, including William Saroyan's *The Cave Dwellers* and the 1957 premiere of Eugene O'Neill's *A Moon for the Misbegotten.* In 1959 the Bijou closed during the renovation and expansion of the adjacent Astor Theatre. This enlargement, which could only be achieved by cutting into the Bijou, cost the small playhouse half its seats and all its wing space stage left. (The Bijou's other neighbor, the Morosco, had always suffered from a tiny lobby. Plans were also drawn up to use part of the Bijou for an expanded entrance for the Morosco, but they were ultimately dropped.) The wounded theatre reopened in 1962 as the D.W. Griffith, a 300-seat cinema for art films. Japanese features took over in 1963, an occasion for which the theatre was renamed the Toho Cinema. The original name was restored in 1965, but movies remained the fare until 1970 when *Foreplay,* a homosexual drama, briefly returned live theatre to the Bijou. After a couple more years of movies, the Bijou was cleaned up for another stab at live drama. *The Enemy is Dead* bombed in 1973, and so did the six shows that followed. But in 1977 the Bijou hit it big hosting an unusual Swiss enter-

LEFT : Bijou Theatre, 1926. To the right is the stage house of the Astor. (TX)

ABOVE : Bijou Theatre interior, 1917. (AB)

tainment called *Mummenschanz.* A family show featuring mime, music, and masks, *Mummenschanz* set the house record of 1,326 performances during its three-year run.

Unfortunately, the next four shows at the Bijou weren't as attractive to ticket-buyers as the playhouse itself was to developers. The Bijou was one of five theatres standing in the way of a new luxury hotel. When the courts permitted partial clearing of the site in 1982, the Bijou was the first to go.

ABOVE : The Morosco and Bijou Theatres in 1919. (LC)

ABOVE : The same view in 1974. The space used by the ticket agency was carved from the Bijou's lobby and auditorium. (NvH)

NORWORTH THEATRE

125 WEST 48TH STREET EUGENE DE ROSA, 1918

On 28 January 1918 an intimate new theatre opened just east of the Playhouse on 48th Street. Seating little more than 500, the building's contribution to the history of Broadway was minor at best. Jack Norworth was an actor, producer, and occasional husband and partner of Nora Bayes (who, at the end of 1918, would have her own theatre on the roof of the 44th Street). His stage successes revealed his ability to gauge the public's taste, a skill that was evident as well in the building that he opened. Critics called the Norworth "one of the city's prettiest and most comfortable playhouses"—flattery they bestowed on almost every new theatre. Built on a plot 56 feet x 100 feet, the Norworth's handsome brick facade was lit by two large lanterns mounted on each side of the arched window that curved over the marquee. Boasting a single balcony, two proscenium boxes, wall murals, and simple furnishings in blue, oak, and gold, the Norworth's interior design was subtle and refined. To open the Norworth, *Odds and Ends* of 1917 moved from the Bijou. The decision to christen the new theatre with a transfer show was an unusual but understandable one, as Norworth was both the star and producer of the revue. His new career as theatre manager was as short as the eight-week run of *Odds and Ends.* When the revue closed Norworth lost his theatre. The house was barely four months old when the new managers renamed it the Belmont. After productions of *Crops and Croppers* and *I.O.U.* flopped at the Belmont, the managers booked a season of French drama in 1919, renaming the playhouse Theatre Parisien in the process. The novelty wore off quickly, though, and by 1920 the house was again known as the Belmont. It was another year before the house booked a show of any note. *Miss Lulu Bett* won the Pulitzer Prize of 1921 and was the Belmont's first hit attraction. In 1923 playwright Philip Barry made his Broadway debut at the Belmont with *You and I,* another success for the theatre. Three years later the Belmont's biggest hit arrived, a revue called *Americana.* Charles Butterworth, Helen Morgan, and Betty Compton starred in the witty satire for 224 performances.) The thirties started off promisingly enough with a comedy called *Stepping Sisters,* the saga of ex-burlesque queens. But critical and public response warranted a move to a larger house, leaving the Belmont to play host to a series of flops. Hit hard by the depression, the house shuttered in 1933 and remained dark for three years. *In The Bag* brought the Belmont back to the legitimate scene in 1937, but the play only managed four performances. The same year the Belmont was sold in foreclosure to Joan of Arc Pictures for $190,000. Used as a cinema for foreign films, the Belmont occassionaly booked a live show, but success continued to elude the house. By the time it was demolished and replaced with commercial buildings in 1951, it had been a movie theatre for the better part of a decade.

ABOVE : Norworth interior, 1917. (AB)

LEFT : The Norworth Theatre in the mid-twenties. The house was renamed the Belmont just four months after it opened.

ABOVE : Vanderbilt Theatre, 1918. (TX)

VANDERBILT THEATRE

148 WEST 48TH STREET EUGENE DE ROSA, 1918

In the spring of 1918 producer Lyle Andrews built a theatre on West 48th Street to be used for his own productions. John Cort's theatre to the east, H.H. Frazee's Longacre to the west, and William Brady's 48th Street and Playhouse theatres across the street served the same purpose for their producer-builders. The addition of Andrews' Vanderbilt Theatre to this prestigious neighborhood meant that each night 780 more seats were available to people determined to see drama on West 48th Street. Andrews opened the Vanderbilt on March 7th with the musical *Oh, Look,* a failure in New York but a hit on its post-Broadway tour. The first smash at the Vanderbilt didn't come until the following October, when Edith Day starred as *Irene.* One of the biggest hits of the decade, the musical held the house record of 670 performances. Nineteen twenty-one saw the American premiere of Eugene O'Neill's *Anna Christie* at the intimate playhouse, followed, after a few modest hits and many quick flops, by a trio of smash musicals. Richard Rodgers and Lorenz Hart contributed the music and lyrics to *The Girl Friend, Peggy Ann,* and *A Connecticut Yankee,* their most successful shows to that time. The house crossed over into the next decade with some minor crowd-pleasers, the last being the 101-performances of *The Plutocrat* in 1930. Twenty-five unsuccessful shows opened and closed at the Vanderbilt during the next five years, costing Andrews his theatre and the theatre its reputation. The chain of flops was broken by Langston Hughes' *Mulatto* in 1935 and Leonard Sillman's 1936 edition of *New Faces,* but the house remained difficult to book. Owner Martin Jones, attempting to make the property more attractive to producers, gave the house a major overhaul in 1938. Much of the renovation was focused on the stage, which at 31 feet wide by 20 feet deep was one of Broadway's smallest. Unable to extend the back wall of the theatre, Jones instead brought the stage forward thirteen feet. The boxes were removed along with four rows of seats, and a new proscenium was installed to frame the enlarged stage. The seats, now numbering 716, and the walls were redecorated in "modern white," putting the final touches on the $30,000 project. Unfortunately, the new Vanderbilt had about as much luck as the old, and in 1939 it was given over to a sure thing–radio. For seven years NBC originated many network broadcasts there, including Fred Waring's popular music program. Producer Mike Todd purchased the Vanderbilt in 1946 and immediately resold it to ABC, which continued to use it as a radio studio. The network sold it to developer Irving Maidman, who returned it to the legitimate stage in 1952. But by now the neighboring theatres that had given so much excitement to 48th Street a generation earlier simply gave the Vanderbilt too much competition. They were bigger, well-maintained, and better-known; the smaller, forgotten Vanderbilt couldn't attract the winners. Maidman tried for two years, but following the brief runs of *Dead Pigeon* and Ruth Draper's one-woman show in 1954 he closed the house. The Vanderbilt came down that June and was replaced by a parking garage. Ironically, the garage was designed by former Shubert architect Herbert J. Krapp. Even today it is most likely that drivers using his garage are going to one of the theatres he designed.

ABOVE : The proscenium of Henry Miller's Theatre, 1929. (LC)

HENRY MILLER'S THEATRE

124 WEST 43RD STREET   H.C. INGALLS, 1918

Actor-manager Henry Miller's 1918 playhouse was considered by students of theatre architecture to be one the most beautiful in New York. Heywood Broun of the *Tribune* called it "a delight . . . the smoking room is certainly the finest in town," and the *Times* wrote that every spectator "was lapped in luxury as seldom before." Lengthy descriptions of the theatre appeared in newspapers and magazines, all of them complimentary. If Miller's taste in plays equaled his taste in playhouses, his theatre was in for a long, successful career. American colonial architecture was rooted in English Georgian designs, and it was in this latter style that Miller had his theatre constructed. The beautifully-proportioned brick and white marble facade of Henry Miller's Theatre boasted large multi-paned windows, low-arched exit courts, and delicate ironwork. Two exit doors flanked the three center glass entrances. The box-office lobby was oval in shape and colored by a mauve glaze painted over warm cream walls, with a floor of black and white marble, and grayish black fixtures finished in a dull gold. The bright blue inner foyer led to the orchestra and to the lounge and balcony stairs. The use of glazes gave an antique look to the warm gray walls of the auditorium, which was illuminated by a large crystal chandelier hung from the ceiling. Amber brocade hangings decorated the walls while the seats were upholstered in matching tapestry. The two-balcony auditorium was intimate; only 404 of its 950 seats were in the orchestra. The backstage area, although absent of the elevators found in larger houses, boasted a high gridiron (allowing for complete raising of large drop curtains), a modern counterweight fly system, and bright, roomy dressing rooms. On both sides of the footlights Henry Miller's Theatre was designed for comfort. The comedy that opened Henry Miller's Theatre on 1 April 1918, *The Fountain of Youth,* was not well-received and gave little indication of the hits that would make the theatre popular. In fact, the first six shows failed to impress the critics, and it seemed as if Miller's charming playhouse was well on its way to becoming a hard-luck house. Fortunately Miller's luck changed with show number seven. *Mis' Nellie of N'Orleans,* a comedy starring Minnie Maddern Fiske, enjoyed a successful four-month run. *La, La, Lucille,* a musical featuring George Gershwin's first complete Broadway score, followed and was also a hit. Its run was cut short by the Actor's Equity strike of 1919, however. At the end of the year, the strike having been settled, Miller himself co-starred with Blanche Bates in a hit comedy, *The Famous Mrs. Fair.* Laurette Taylor, Lillian Gish, Leslie Howard, and Ruth Chatterton kept the Miller's lights on in some less-than-memorable plays for a few years until the theatre's next hit, *Quarantine,* starring Helen Hayes. In 1925 Noel Coward appeared in the four-month run of his play *The Vortex,* which marked his Broadway debut both as actor and author. A year later Holbrook Blinn turned Molnar's *The Play's the Thing* into a 260-performance hit. Nineteen twenty-six was also the year of Henry Miller's death. His family kept control of the theatre, however, with son Gilbert ultimately becoming a respected and successful producer in his own right.

The Henry Miller Theatre crossed over into the thirties with its first true smash, the drama *Journey's End,* and in 1931 Helen Hayes returned in another Molnar fable, *The Good Fairy.* At a time when the majority of Broadway houses were in receivership, closed, or already exploring other options in movies or radio, the Miller was packing them in with another smash. The 1934 comedy *Personal Appearance,* directed by Antoinette Perry, broke the house record with 501 performances. It was followed by another success, the English melodrama *Libel,* directed by Otto Preminger. Thornton Wilder's *Our Town* premiered at the Miller in 1938 but played out most of its run at the Morosco. (The experimental play had been panned during its Boston tryout, prompting Miller to be unsure of its viability in New York. He therefore booked another show to immediately follow it, forcing *Our Town* to move after its successful opening.)  Helen Hayes made her third appearance at Henry Miller's in *Harriet,* the theatre's first long run of the forties. The 1943 biographical drama played 377 times. *The Moon is Blue* was the first hit of the fifties. The comedy gave its premiere performance in 1951 and by the time it closed two-and-a-half years later established a new house record of 924 performances. Bette Davis returned to Broadway for a brief run in 1960's *The World of Carl Sandburg* and Gig Young followed in the comedy *Under the Yum Yum Tree. Enter Laughing,* a 419-performance hit in 1963, proved to be the theatre's last successful booking.

BELOW : Henry Miller's Theatre, 1929. (LC)

ABOVE: Auditorium, 1925. (LC)

In January 1967 the Miller family sold their theatre to the Nederlanders, the Detroit-based theatre operators. Having just adapted the Palace Theatre for legitimate shows, they were looking for other New York properties. Once the Nederlanders agreed to retain the theatre's name, legitimate policy, continue to provide office space for Gilbert Miller, and pay $600,000, the playhouse was theirs. The Nederlanders, though, didn't keep it for very long. In May 1968 they sold it to builder Seymour Durst, who immediately leased it back to them for five years. Off-Broadway's Circle in the Square producers then took a two year sub-lease on the house as they planned to make the move uptown. After the four-performance run of their third flop, *But, Seriously*, the group lost their lease and the house was turned over to movie exhibitor Maurice Maurer for the premiere of Andy Warhol's *Lonesome Cowboy* in March 1969.

As Times Square deteriorated in the early seventies so did the fare on West 43rd Street. Known variously as the Park-Miller or, oddly enough, as the Avon-at-the-Hudson (after the Hudson Theatre closed), the lovely old playhouse became one of the city's most notorious pornographic movie theatres. Despite the outrage of the theatrical community, explicit films ran for five years. In 1977 Durst announced the theatre would be refurbished and returned to legit, but instead it reopened in 1978 as Xenon, a $2 million discotheque. It was as a disco that Henry Miller's presented its last legit show to date. A revival of the comedy *The Ritz* racked up all of one performance in 1983's version of dinner theatre. This, actually, was "disco-theatre," where a ticket to the play entitled patrons to an evening of free disco afterward. It was a trend that did not catch on.

Today, the playhouse still graces 43rd Street with its elegant Georgian facade. Declared an exterior landmark, Henry Miller's Theatre offers people an entertaining night out as a nightclub and discotheque.

RIGHT : As an adult movie house, 1975. (NvH)

ABOVE : The southwest corner of Broadway and 47th Street in 1933. (LC)

CENTRAL THEATRE

1567 Broadway at 47th Street   Herbert J. Krapp, 1918

In the fall of 1918, flush from their successful stage productions and theatre holdings, Lee and J.J. Shubert opened their fifth playhouse in eighteen months on a site directly across from vaudeville's mecca, the Palace. Named for its prime location, the Central Theatre was destined to play only a small part in the history of New York's legitimate stage.   The Central was one of the few playhouses to have an entrance on Broadway. The theatre's lobby extended from the street through the bottom of a five-story brick building. Constructed in the late 19th century, it was once the Mathushek & Son piano factory. The theatre itself was located behind this building on 47th Street, some 100 feet west of Broadway. The doors from the lobby opened to the left side of the auditorium. From there patrons made their way up an aisle to a wide promenade behind the orchestra section, where stairs to the balcony and exits to 47th Street were located.   The interior of the Central was designed by Shubert house architect Herbert J. Krapp in the style of Louis XVI. Decorative wall mouldings, elaborate ornamental plasterwork surrrounding the oval ceiling cove, and cupid-head capitals on the balcony pillars were highlighted in shades of colored French gray and old gold. The theatre was bigger than average, seating an audience of 1,100 in its orchestra, balcony, and boxes. Despite the ample space in front of the footlights, the stage was a rather shallow twenty-five feet deep, and the proscenium opening a relatively narrow thirty feet wide. These dimensions made the Central's stage one of Broadway's smallest, and possibly one of its least desirable.   The play *Forever After* opened the Central on 9 September 1918. Starring Conrad Nagel and Alice Brady, *Forever After* was performed successfully 312 times. But it was not until 1920 that the theatre earned its place in the record books. In February of that year a poorly received musical titled *Always You* closed at the Central following its 66th performance. Among the show's creators was 24 year-old book writer and lyricist Oscar Hammerstein II, who was making his Broadway debut. Six months later another musical at the Central gave two young hopefuls their first chance to write a complete Broadway score. *Poor Little Ritz Girl* began its 119-performance run in July 1920, and started 18 year-old Richard Rodgers and 25 year-old Lorenz Hart on their way to creating some of the musical theatre's most popular songs. (Rodgers and Hart returned to the Central four years later with the flop *The Melody Man,* a play with songs such as "I'd Like to Poison Ivy (Because She Clings to Me)." The pair managed to keep their names off this minor effort.)   The Central had a variety of other shows during its first decade, including *As You Were,* a revue with an early Cole Porter lyric, and the comedy *Solid Ivory.* It even had a brief affair with motion pictures when Universal leased it for a year in 1921. Following *That French Lady* in 1927, the affair became a marriage when the Central joined the growing number of Times Square theatres devoted exclusively to movies.

ABOVE : Central Theatre, 1917. (NYHS)

onnie's Inn Revue brought some life back to the Central's stage in 1932. But the theatre's entertainments became a bit too risqué for city officials in July of that year when Minsky's Burlesque took over. Although the theatre reverted to films three months later, burlesque made a comeback in 1933 when it was combined with screen shows. For two months in 1934, burlesque went full-time at the theatre, which was renamed the Columbia for the occasion. By May, however, movies and the old name were back.

In 1942, the Central briefly offered burlesque-like revues called "mirror-girl shows," but business was bad and the house returned to grinding out second-run films. The theatre's name was changed to the Gotham in 1944 and it remained a movie theatre for the next seven years. In 1951 the theatre closed for renovation, reopening with a new name, the Holiday, and a live stage revue, *Bagels and Yox*. A second show, a nightclub variety called *A Night in Havana*, followed in 1952. It was described as a "peep show" by an association of Broadway businessmen who were worried that the Holiday varieties would pave the way for the return of burlesque to Times Square. After an absence of nearly thirty years, legitimate plays once again appeared on the stage of the theatre. *Deadfall*, starring Joanne Dru and John Ireland, began the new policy in 1955. Others followed, but by 1957 the house was offering striptease instead of Shakespeare, and shortly thereafter it reverted to showing movies. Known as the Odeon, the Forum, the Forum 47th Street, and finally as Movieland, films kept the old showplace open through 1988. The Shuberts, who had owned the Central since its construction, sold it in the spring of 1989. The lobby was converted into the Roxy deli and the theatre behind it was rebuilt as a disco called Club USA. In 1995 the nightclub was evicted for non-payment of rent and a short time later the deli also closed. The following year the property was sold at auction to the Banque Nationale de Paris for an astonishing $31 million, signaling renewed investor confidence in Times Square. The two buildings stand vacant and closed in 1997, their demolition likely but not yet definite.

ABOVE : Central Theatre interior, 1917. (AB)

ABOVE : Central Theatre interior, 1989. (NvH)

BELOW : Balcony detail, 1989. (NvH)

SELWYN THEATRE

229 WEST 42ND STREET GEORGE KEISTER, 1918

Producers Edgar and Arch Selwyn somehow found enough space on crowded 42nd Street to open the block's tenth theatre in 1918. Their playhouse was constructed behind the Selwyn Building, a six-story office tower with a multi-windowed light terra-cotta facade. The first floor of the building was devoted to lobbies and lounges extending 100 feet to the body of the theatre on 43rd Street, where the simple brick facade was in stark contrast to the delicate Renaissance design of the main entrance. The auditorium was also a treatment of early Italian Renaissance style. Antique Alps Green and Pavaonazao marbles formed the base of the single-balcony interior. The walls, colored in old Italian blue and antique gold, were decorated with five large mural paintings. The two floors and eight boxes accommodated 1,100 persons in seats upholstered in a blue fabric that matched the color of the stage curtain and auditorium draperies.

A comedy co-authored by and starring Jane Cowl, *Information, Please,* opened the Selwyn Theatre on 2 October 1918. Despite Miss Cowl's popularity, the play proved to be an unlucky choice for the Selwyn's premiere when it flopped after just 46 performances. The actress immediately returned in the theatre's second show, *The Crowded Hour,* and managed to triple the length of her previous stay. The Selwyn's first true hits were 1919's *Buddies,* a musical starring Peggy Wood, and the following year's *Tickle Me,* a comedy. In September 1921 Mrs. Leslie Carter, a Broadway star at the turn of the century, returned to the stage to join John Drew, another larger-than-life performer, in Somerset Maugham's *The Circle.*

George S. Kaufman and Marc Connelly brought their musical *Helen of Troy, New York* to the Selwyn for six months in 1923. Two years after Beatrice Lillie, Gertrude Lawrence, and Jack Buchanan starred in the *Charlot Revue,* Kaufman returned to the Selwyn with what proved to be the playhouse's biggest hit. *The Royal Family,* co-written with Edna Ferber, was a biting satire of the on- and off-stage theatrics of the Drews and Barrymores. While the subjects of the play were not amused, audiences most definitely were, keeping the show alive for 345 performances.

There were three more bright spots in the Selwyn's history before it began its slide into grind movies that none of the 42nd Street houses escaped. Bea Lillie returned to co-star with Noel Coward in his 1928 revue *This Year of Grace;* Cole Porter scored in 1929 with another revue, *Wake Up and Dream;* and Fred Allen, Clifton Webb, and Fred MacMurray crossed over into the new decade in the popular Dietz and Schwartz musical *Three's A Crowd.* None of the next eleven shows was a hit; some, like 1931's *The Singing Rabbi,* ran less than a week. The failure of *Ragged Army* in 1934 was the last straw. Out went costly reserved seats and in went a movie screen and depression-era prices.

Movies had been grinding out at the Selwyn for sixteen years when an unusual new policy was implemented in 1950. The house returned to legitimate theatre for a condensed version of Sartre's *The Respectful Prostitute.* The sixty-minute drama was performed five times a day preceding each showing of the feature film. Three actresses

ABOVE : Selwyn interior, 1918. (AB)

ABOVE : With the exception of the Times Square, all of the 42nd Street theatres had intact stages despite their years of disuse. Some, like the Selwyn, even retained their original light boards and rigging until the equipment was updated during restoration. (MH)

alternated in the lead roles while members of the supporting cast each gave thirty performances a week. This experiment lasted for one more show, a tabloid play called *Ladies Night in a Turkish Bath*. Soon audiences looking for a stage/screen combo had to settle for the Rockettes and first-run films at Radio City Music Hall. Meanwhile the Selwyn reverted to celluloid double-features, a policy that continued into the nineties.

Live theatre returned to the stage of the Selwyn when the Wooster Group's production of Eugene O'Neill's *The Hairy Ape* began a limited run in March 1997. As the redevelopment of 42nd Street continues, the Selwyn is slated for restoration as the block's second not-for-profit playhouse (the New Victory is the first) and new home of the Roundabout Theatre.

ABOVE : Selwyn auditorium, 1997. (NvH)

ABOVE : Times Square Theatre rendering, 1920. (LC)

TIMES SQUARE THEATRE

219 WEST 42ND STREET   EUGENE DE ROSA, 1920

Edgar and Arch Selwyn expanded their presence on 42nd Street by opening two new theatres in the fall of 1920. The Times Square and the Apollo were the ninth and tenth playhouses to light up 42nd Street. They were also the last, bringing to a close three decades of entrepreneurial spirit that turned a quiet residential street into the brightest block of the Great White Way. A limestone facade with an open colonnade gave the Times Square an elegant street appearance while also providing an entrance to the Apollo's long, narrow lobby. The Times Square's lobby, however, was quite small and opened directly to a promenade behind the 512 orchestra seats. The capacity of the single balcony exceeded that of the orchestra by seventeen; the four boxes brought the theatre's total capacity to 1,057. The auditorium, described by the *Times* as "simple, spacious, handsome, comfortable," was Empire in style and colored in tones of green, silver, and black. Murals and ornamental plasterwork provided most of the interior decoration. The tapestried seats were in stark contrast to the black carpet and black velvet house curtain. Edgar Selwyn christened the Times Square with his own play, *The Mirage*, which began a six-month stay on September 30, 1920. The eight-month run of *The Demi-Virgin* dominated the theatre's second season, but the third year saw only two unsuccessful musicals. The 1923–24 season featured appearances by Tallulah Bankhead, Robert Cummings, and, in their American debuts, Gertrude Lawrence and Beatrice Lillie. Jerome Kern's *Dear Sir* flopped in 1924, but the following year Channing Pollock's *The Enemy* managed 203 showings. Eighteen more shows opened at the Times Square between 1926 and 1933. The four hits not only entertained audiences of the day but still prove to be potent draws over half a century later. *Gentlemen Prefer Blondes* chalked up 199 performances in the 1926-27 season and was the basis for the smash musical of the same name. In 1928 Charles MacArthur and Ben Hecht's *The Front Page* transported audiences to a wisecracking Chicago newsroom. The comedy hit established the house record of 276 performances. In 1930 George Gershwin urged everyone to *Strike Up the Band*, and the following year Noel Coward aimed his wit at the follies of the upper classes in *Private Lives*. Gertrude Lawrence, Laurence Olivier, and Coward himself starred in the comedy, which played 256 times. In the summer of 1933 the Times Square went dark following Tallulah Bankhead's thirteen-week run in *Forsaking All Others*, only to reopen the next year as a movie house. Six years later a retail store was constructed on its stage, making a return to live theatre an expensive and difficult proposition. As of 1997, the Times Square is in relatively good condition but closed, waiting for a tenant who will likely adapt the theatre into a retail or restaurant space while preserving its elegant design.

TIMES SQUARE THEATRE

ABOVE : 42nd Street, 1989. (MH)

ABOVE : Times Square auditorium, 1920. (AB)

ABOVE : Times Square auditorium, 1997. For years a movie screen hid the brick wall of a store that had been built in place of the stage. (NvH)

APOLLO THEATRE

223 WEST 42ND STREET EUGENE DE ROSA, 1920

As legitimate theatres were springing up all over Times Square, the Bryant opened as 42nd Street's first film and vaudeville house in 1910. A decade later the Selwyn brothers, who operated a successful playhouse down the street, took over the property and rebuilt it as a legitimate theatre sharing a common facade with their new Times Square Theatre. Christened the Apollo, it was the twelfth and final showplace to open on the block that for a brief time flourished as the theatre center of the world. A long, narrow lobby of Belgian and Italian marbles was entered from 42nd Street under a marquee the Apollo shared with the adjacent Times Square Theatre. The auditorium, on the 43rd Street side of the block, was decorated in shades of tan, rose, and blue and boasted a brilliant peacock blue velvet house curtain. The orchestra could seat 675, the boxes 24, and the balcony, with the first cross-over aisle in the city, accommodated 495, for a total capacity of 1,194. The stage, with its modern system of counterweights and elevators, would easily handle the musicals that were to call the Apollo home. The Apollo Theatre did not begin its legitimate career with much success. Oscar Hammerstein II contributed to the script and score of the theatre's first production, *Jimmie.* Its 71 performances started on 11 November 1920. Lionel Barrymore's interpretation of *Macbeth* began the new year off with promise, but it was followed by five failures. In the fall of 1923 the Apollo booked its first hit, *Poppy,* starring W.C. Fields. *George White's Scandals of 1924,* with a Gershwin score, continued the Apollo's winning streak. White was a frequent tenant of the theatre, booking five subsequent editions of his popular revue at the Apollo and setting the house record with the 424 performances of *Scandals of 1926.* Ethel Merman, Helen Morgan, Willie and Eugene Howard, Ann Pennington, Jimmy Durante, Ray Bolger, and Rudy Vallee were among White's stars, although the choruses of undressed show-girls proved to be equally potent draws. In between the annual *Scandals* a number of popular book musicals premiered at the Apollo. Ed Wynn starred in *Manhattan Mary* 264 times in 1927, and Bert Lahr, Kate Smith, and the alliterative Gale Quadruplets (Jane, Jean, June, and Joan) were *Flying High* for 357 performances in 1930. Two years later *Take A Chance* cast Ethel Merman with Jack Whiting and Jack Haley. It was followed by *Blackbirds of 1933,* a 25-performance flop and the Apollo's final legitimate show for nearly forty-five years. The Apollo remained empty until November 1934, when it was recruited as the latest Times Square burlesque house. In 1938 foreign films took over the theatre; thirty years later action movies lit up the screen. In 1978 the Brandt Organization, in a bold attempt to return live theatre to its 42nd Street houses, closed the Apollo and began the clean-up necessary to attract legitimate producers. New seats and chandeliers were installed, and the entrance was moved away from tawdry 42nd Street to 43rd Street, where a new marquee announced the first booking at the New Apollo, *On Golden Pond.* The 1979 play enjoyed a modest run, as did the two shows that followed: *Bent,*

LEFT : Apollo Theatre, 1921. The other side of the marquee announced attractions at the Times Square Theatre, which shared a common facade with the Apollo. (LC)

starring Richard Gere, and *The Fifth of July*. After *The Guys in the Truck* flopped in 1983, however, the theatre reverted to the silver screen. The Apollo's final incarnation was as the Academy, a venue for rock concerts. But in 1996, once the bands had stopped playing, all significant architectural elements were removed and the theatre was demolished. The rescued proscenium, boxes, ceiling dome, and other plasterwork will be restored and reused in a new theatre, the Ford Center for the Performing Arts. Set to open in 1998, it will be constructed on the combined sites of the Lyric and Apollo theatres. (See page 257 for sections of the theatres before and after restoration as the Ford Center.)

LEFT : Apollo interior, 1932. (TH)

BELOW : Apollo lobby during the 1924 run of *George White's Scandal's*. (TH)

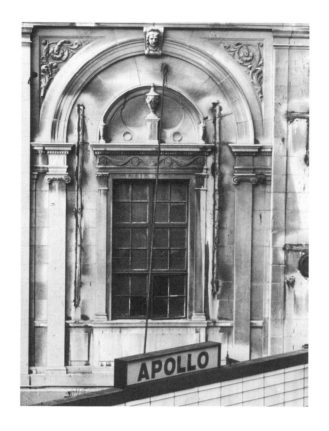

ABOVE : Apollo Theatre's 43rd Street facade in 1990. It was demolished six years later. (NvH)

LEFT : The Apollo's 42nd Street facade, which it shared with the Times Square Theatre, in 1989. Floor plans for both theatres appear on page 270. (MH)

BELOW : Apollo interior, 1989. As the Academy, the orchestra seats were replaced with a dance floor. (MH)

KLAW THEATRE

Marc Klaw and Abe Erlanger were two of the most powerful men in the theatre at the turn of the century. Along with five other managers they formed a syndicate to bring order to the chaotic business of booking theatres outside New York. In no time they had created a monopoly. Any producer who had a show to tour was forced to go through the syndicate, as was the manager of any available out-of-town playhouse. Although the arrival of the Shubert brothers helped to break up the syndicate's monopoly, Klaw and Erlanger, both as partners and individually, remained powerful forces in the industry. Like other leading producers, each built his own theatre—Erlanger's (now the St. James) on West 44th Street and the Klaw one block north.   **T**he exterior of the Klaw Theatre was a beautiful combination of three of the more popular building materials of the period. Colonial in design, the facade featured red brick laid in panels of contrasting patterns. Gray granite formed the base of the building, while the cornice, pilasters, and arches over the three large windows were of architectural terra-cotta. The lobby featured wainscoting of Italian marble and a terrazzo floor. The auditorium accommodated 806, making the house ideal for intimate comedies and dramas. The primary color scheme of the orchestra and single balcony was gray and gold with highlights of blue, and both levels featured paneled wood wainscoting. A chandelier suspended from the large flat dome cast a warm glow on the rich plaster ornamentation of the boxes and proscenium arch. At the rear of the orchestra section twin marble staircases led up to the single balcony and mezzanine offices and down to the Elizabethan-style basement lounge. Here patrons could enjoy the warmth of a fire burning in a large stone hearth in a room decorated in gray stucco and dark oak panels.   **T**he Klaw Theatre was welcomed to Broadway with two back-to-back comedy hits. *Nice People,* featuring Katharine Cornell and Tallulah Bankhead, christened the theatre on 2 March 1921. Critics praised the play and the playhouse, although one noted that the plaster walls were still damp. *Lillies of the Field* followed in October and was presented 169 times. Later seasons saw Humphrey Bogart and Clifton Webb co-starring in the 232-performance comedy *Meet the Wife,* George Abbott in the 1923 Pulitzer Prize-winning drama *Hell-Bent fer Heaven,* and a Theatre Guild production of *Androcles and the Lion.*   **A**fter two years of flops, the Klaw came back in September 1928 with a new name and a huge hit. Brock Pemberton renamed the house the Avon for his production of Preston Sturges' comedy *Strictly Dishonorable,* which ultimately became the theatre's long-run champ with 557 performances. It also was the Avon's final hit. **A**lthough many noteworthy productions booked the Avon (including a revival of Noel Coward's *Hay Fever* and Cornelia Otis Skinner's portrayal of all of *The Wives of Henry VIII*), none of them was a success. In the spring of 1934 the management of the theatre was approached by executives of the Columbia Broadcasting System. The young network had grown tremendously and, in spite of having leased the Hudson Theatre, was in need of more studio space large enough to accommodate an audience. For the Avon it

ABOVE : In a 1935 snapshot the view of the north side of 45th Street included the CBS Radio Playhouse (formerly the Klaw) and the Imperial, Music Box, and Morosco theatres. (LC)

was a guarantee of steady income in the depressing days of bankrupt theatres. The lease was signed and the Avon was renamed CBS Radio Playhouse No. 2. Three years later CBS bought the house outright, and continued to base many of its network radio programs there well into the fifties.

In 1953 CBS sold the Avon to Abraham and Frederick Dreier, two brothers who operated a chain of hotels. The Dreiers planned to take advantage of changes in the building code and construct a hotel above the theatre. While this project was being studied they made the Avon available to outside producers, with the provision that whoever booked the theatre would bear the cost of restoring it to its pre-radio condition. Although producers were lined up to book a house in the heart of 45th Street, none would agree to the Dreiers' terms. Not surprisingly, the Avon stood vacant. By 1954 the Dreiers had decided that perhaps the site could be used more profitably and the Avon was demolished. The parking structure that went up in its place still stands.

ABOVE : Marble staircase leading to the Klaw's balcony, 1921. (AB)

LEFT : Proscenium, 1921. (TH)

BELOW : Klaw Theatre exterior, 1921. (AB)

ABOVE : Jolson's 59th Street Theatre, 1922. (SA)

JOLSON'S 59TH STREET THEATRE

932 SEVENTH AVENUE   HERBERT J. KRAPP, 1921

During the early years of the Shubert's theatrical empire, Lee and J.J. periodically honored their biggest stars by naming new theatres after them. Maxine Elliott, Joe Weber and Lew Fields, Alla Nazimova, and Ethel Barrymore gratefully performed for the Shuberts at their namesake playhouses between 1908 and 1928. After enjoying the considerable profits of Al Jolson's frequent Winter Garden engagements, the Shuberts decided it was time to honor him with a theatre of his own. Although they had planned to call their latest theatre the Imperial, the Shuberts enthusiastically renamed it Jolson's 59th Street once Jolson himself agreed to star in the opening production. But in their excitement Lee and J.J. neglected one thing. The theatre was actually on 58th Street, with Seventh Avenue the location of its main entrance. Perhaps they took a few liberties with the address so the theatre could be associated with one of Manhattan's more fashionable streets, which 59th at Central Park was and still is. Or, maybe they just made a mistake. Built on the site of the old Central Park Riding Academy, Jolson's was on the edge of the theatre district. One of the largest houses, it could accommodate over 1,700 persons in the orchestra, balcony, and boxes. The huge stage, 80 feet x 45 feet, was ideally suited for the most elaborate productions of the era. The bright interior, which was considered rather ordinary by many critics, featured variegated trimmings in the style of the late 1890s and a curved acoustic ceiling. True to his word, Al Jolson opened his theatre with the musical *Bombo* on 6 October 1921. The show was a tremendous hit in New York and on tour and earned the Shuberts a profit of nearly half-a-million dollars. But despite his success at the uptown showplace, Jolson never again appeared there. After *Bombo*, Jolson's presented many popular productions, including *The Student Prince, My Maryland* (both scored by *Bombo*'s composer Sigmund Romberg), and the team of E.H. Southern and Julia Marlowe in a repertory of Shakespeare's plays. In 1923 came the theatre's most memorable engagement, the twelve-week American premiere of Constantin Stanislavsky's Moscow Art Theatre. The acting method his company displayed in *The Cherry Orchard, Three Sisters,* and *The Brothers Karamazov* is still studied today. In its tenth year, when the depression robbed Jolson's of its solvency, the house turned to a policy of films under a new name, the Central Park. In 1932 Shakespeare's classics returned in the form of fifteen separate productions aimed at student audiences. A total of 249 performances, priced from a quarter to a dollar, were given at the theatre, which was renamed the Shakespeare for the occasion. The building was known as the Venice when the operetta *Africana* managed three performances in 1934. Movies and weekend recitals followed, but the house was dark for months at a stretch. In 1937 Orson Welles literally marched his production of *The Cradle Will Rock* into the Venice. Welles and John Houseman planned to open the labor opera at Maxine Elliott's Theatre, but two hours before the first public performance the Federal Theatre Administration, afraid the show might embarass the government, pulled the plug. Houseman hastily booked the empty Venice and moved the waiting audience forty blocks north. Under orders from Actor's Equity not to perform on stage, the cast bought tickets and delivered their lines from their seats while composer Marc Blitzen played a rented piano on the bare stage. It was an unforgettable night. *The Cradle Will Rock* played nineteen times at the Venice before moving elsewhere for a regular engagement. Vacant once again, the theatre was taken over by the Yiddish Art Players for the next five years. The house resurfaced in 1942 as Jolson's for *Comes A Revelation,* a two-performance turkey. Subsequently Molly Picon brought Yiddish plays back to the theatre, which in true Shubert fashion was renamed in her honor. The name "Jolson" was back on the marquee in 1943 when the deteriorating theatre switched to foreign language movies.

ABOVE : Jolson's interior, 1922. (SA)

The playhouse's slide into oblivion was stopped by a severe shortage of theatres large enough to accommodate musicals. The Shuberts completely refurbished the house in 1944, renamed it the New Century (the old Century having been demolished fourteen years earlier), and booked many hits into it. *Follow the Girls* with Jackie Gleason, *Up in Central Park*, Phil Silvers in *High Button Shoes,* and the Bea Lillie revue *Inside U.S.A.* kept the Century's lights on season after season. In 1948 the ongoing theatre shortage forced Cole Porter's *Kiss Me, Kate* into the Century, where it set the house record of 1,070 performances. *Out of This World* and *Don Juan in Hell* followed, but by the early fifties the Century was less in demand as the shortage eased.

Following the brief 1953 run of *Carnival in Flanders* starring John Raitt and Dolores Gray, the Century closed. In 1954 NBC leased it for $100,000 a year and turned it into one of their many midtown studios. When the network moved out five years later, the theatre remained a television facility, the independently operated Video Tape Center.

The Shubert Organization sold the Century in 1962. It was demolished that year and replaced with an apartment building.

ABOVE : Jolson's interior, 1922. (SA)

49TH STREET THEATRE

235 WEST 49TH STREET   HERBERT J. KRAPP, 1921

The Shuberts' second theatre on 49th Street was a small, handsome playhouse reminiscent of the Booth. Unlike that successful theatre, however, the 49th Street stayed in the legitimate fold only seventeen years; by the outbreak of World War II it had vanished from the scene completely. The 49th Street Theatre followed the Renaissance style of design. Pilasters and the large cornice they supported were the primary elements of the white marble facade. Five doors led into a lobby that was spacious in proportion to the rest of the house. In order to maximize the number of seats and still provide for the necessary exit courts, Shubert architect Herbert J. Krapp ingeniously placed the egg-shaped auditorium at an angle to the street. This created the courts in a space which otherwise would have been too narrow to allow for the final capacity of 750. The decorations of the auditorium suggested the intimate atmosphere of an old English drawing room. The walls of the orchestra and single balcony were paneled in rich oak and crowned with subdued gray plasterwork. The ceiling was ivory, and the fabric of the curtain and seats was in matching tones of antique blue. An unsuccessful comedy, *Face Value,* opened the 49th Street the day after Christmas in 1921. The 1922 Russian vaudeville *Chauve-Souris* was the second attraction and the theatre's first hit. It played 153 times before moving to the Century Roof Theatre for the summer. The 44-week run of *Whispering Wires* established the house record in 1923, but the following year *Gypsy Jim,* a play by Oscar Hammerstein II, flopped after only six weeks. The next few seasons produced notable performances by Katharine Cornell, Lionel Atwill, Leslie Howard, Fay Bainter, and Estelle Winwood (the latter two in Noel Coward's *Fallen Angels*). By the time the Shuberts lost the 49th Street in the depression it had been years since a real hit had opened there. When the Shubert fortunes reversed, Lee and J.J. expressed no interest in regaining control of the small playhouse. The failures continued to mount in the thirties, culminating in Irving Stone's *Truly Valiant* (one performance in 1936) and Rex Ingram in *How Come, Lawd?* (two performances the following year). After three plays by the Federal Theatre Project in 1937 and three performances of a modern dress version of *The Wild Duck* in 1938, the stage of the 49th Street went dark. A screen and speakers were installed and the house reopened as Cinema 49. Its career as a movie theatre was brief, however, and by the end of 1940 it was decided to make better use out of the small plot on West 49th Street. That December the pretty little playhouse that had proved so unpopular with modern audiences was demolished.

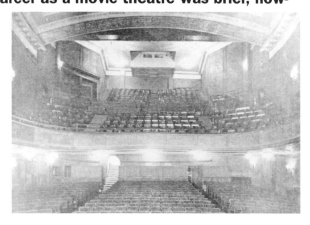

LEFT : The 49th Street Theatre nearing completion in 1921. (HK)

RIGHT : Interior, 1921. The irregular shape of the balcony is due to the auditorium's angle to 49th Street. (AB)

ABOVE : The rebuilt Earl Carroll Theatre, southeast corner of Seventh Avenue and 50th Street, 1931. (NYHS)

EARL CARROLL THEATRE

753 Seventh Avenue George Keister, 1923•George Keister & Joseph Babolnay, 1931

Mix a talented young entreprenuer with a Texas millionaire, add scores of beautiful women, two brand-new Broadway theatres and a prohibition scandal that ended in federal prison, and you have the rollercoaster career of songwriter, producer, inventor, and creator of the *Vanities,* Earl Carroll. **C**arroll was six months shy of thirty when his first Broadway theatre opened in 1922, courtesy of funds from Texas oil millionaire Colonel William R. Edrington. (The producer found his investor by running an ad in a New York newspaper. They remained business associates until Carroll's second theatre drove the Colonel into bankruptcy.) **T**he main entrance to the Earl Carroll Theatre was through the ground floor of a nondescript six-story brick building on Seventh Avenue, while the auditorium and stage fronted 50th Street. The playhouse, designed in the style of the Italian Renaissance, had room for 1,026 in its orchestra and single balcony, and was notable for being one of the district's first theatres to omit boxes from its plan. In place of the boxes Carroll built two identical stage platforms to be used for curtain calls or scenes from the play itself. The interior color scheme was also a departure from the norm with the primary tone being a luminous turquoise blue accented by antique burnished gold. The functions of the house curtain were performed by three separate drops. The first, made of iridescent silk with highlights of rose, blue, and hyacinth, extended sixteen feet into the auditorium, concealing the orchestra pit. When the curtain opened the orchestra would rise into view (thanks to hydraulic lifts) and the middle drop would part, leaving the individual act curtain revealed and providing a very theatrical start to each performance. **B**ehind the scenes, the Earl Carroll boasted many innovations in stagecraft including new lighting and counterweight systems. The most dramatic of them was the only Broadway application of the permanent hard cyclorama. The back wall of the theatre was finished with a concave, smooth plaster surface painted a neutral gray. Dubbed a "horizant," it allowed for any number of lighting effects, from a bright blue sky to the infinity of an ocean horizon on a cloudy day. Since performers were unable to pass from one side of the stage to the other behind the wall, a cross-over trench was built directly in front of it. In the wings were a green room, complete with fireplace, and a marble staircase leading to the tiers of dressing rooms above the stage. **D**espite the innovations, the Earl Carroll opened with a bomb of Mr. Carroll's own device. *Bavu,* a Russian melodrama that ran less than a month, featured Carlotta Monterey (the third Mrs. Eugene O'Neill) and newcomer William Powell in its cast. *Just Because,* a musical starring Queenie Smith, was the Carroll's second booking and also a failure. **J**ust as Colonel Edrington must have been having doubts about his association with Carroll, the producer hit the jackpot with *White Cargo,* a sultry South Seas drama he opened at Daly's 63rd Street Theatre. It ran in New York and on the road for years. In August 1922 the Earl Carroll had its first hit, a musical called *The Gingham Girl.* It stayed at the theatre for eight months.

Carroll's winning streak continued when he started a series of revues that would give him hit after hit for nearly a decade. Flo Ziegfeld had glorified the American girl in the *Follies;* now Carroll honored the most beautiful women in the world in his *Vanities of 1923.* Like Ziegfeld's *Follies* and George White's *Scandals,* Earl Carroll's *Vanities* featured sketches, songs, and production numbers with dozens of women in various states of undress. Ziegfeld put more emphasis on wardrobe; Carroll on its absence. While the *Follies* was generally regarded as the superior revue, each

BELOW : Earl Carroll auditorium, 1930. (LC)

was able to find an audience in the days before radio and television. Following the run of the first *Vanities* Ziegfeld booked his competitor's theatre for *Kid Boots.* Both tenant and landlord profited handsomely from the Eddie Cantor musical.

ABOVE : Proscenium of the first Earl Carroll Theatre, 1930. (LC)

With the exception of occasional dramas such as O'Neill's *Desire Under the Elms,* the Carroll was primarily used for annual editions of the *Vanities.* The production to get the most attention, however, took place after a performance of Carroll's lavish revue. On 22 February 1926, Carroll threw a birthday bash for the "father of his theatre," Colonel Edrington. Among the 200 guests admitted through the stage door were columnists Ed Sullivan and Walter Winchell, Harry K. Thaw (just released from a mental institution after murdering Stanford White), and of course a bevy of scantily-clad chorus beauties. The highlight of the party came at dawn, when a bathtub containing gallons of champagne and one nude chorus girl was wheeled on stage. Carroll encouraged all to dip their cups and drink a toast to the Colonel. In the Grand Jury investigation that followed (this was, after all, prohibition) Carroll denied the events of the 22nd had taken place. For this testimony he was ultimately convicted of perjury and served six months in a federal prison.

Upon his release Carroll picked up where he left off. His theatre presented the *Earl Carroll Vanities of 1928* (this time with Ziegfeld's former star W.C. Fields), followed in 1929 by *Fioretta.* Financed by a friend of the composers, Carroll wrote the operetta's book and staged it. Despite having Fanny Brice and Leon Errol in the cast, the $350,000 *Fioretta* proved to be the most expensive Broadway failure of the times. After *Fioretta* closed, the seven year-old theatre presented its final show and its biggest hit. *Earl Carroll's Sketchbook* was little more than the *Vanities* under a different name. But the comedy antics of its stars Will Mahoney and Patsy Kelly, plus written contributions from Eddie Cantor, enabled it to become the longest running show of the season with 400 performances.

ABOVE : Earl Carroll proscenium, 1931. The colored house lights were controlled from a special booth downstage of the orchestra pit. (NYHS)

ABOVE : Dramatic lounge under the balcony. (NYHS)

Following the run of *Sketch-book,* Carroll leased his theatre to Radio Pictures while finalizing a plan to triple its size. Since the opening of the Roxy movie palace across the street, the site of the Carroll was considered a highly desirable location for another huge picture house. With a larger theatre Carroll would be able to offer stage or screen shows at competitive prices. After securing the necessary funds from his Texas angel, plus parcels of land directly east and south of his theatre, the Earl Carroll was demolished in 1930.

All that remained was a gutted lobby, the Seventh Avenue facade, and a promise to build the most spectacular theatre Broadway had ever seen. One year and $4.5 million later, Carroll demonstrated his faith in the post-crash economy by unveiling a showplace with room for three-thousand patrons at a top ticket price of three dollars (fifty cents for balcony). Now the most beautiful girls in the world would be available to all at popular prices.

The new Earl Carroll Theatre was Manhattan's largest playhouse and arguably its most spectacular. From the front lobby to the stage door, Broadway's first and only Art Deco theatre was a masterpiece of modern design. A ticket counter of highly polished black vitrolite trimmed in chrome-nickel steel took the place of the standard box office windows. Illumination for the lobby came from lights concealed in a cove below a white vitrolite dome. Directly off the ticket lobby was the 4,000 square foot main foyer decorated in polished black cement (called "burkstone"), plaster, steel, and aluminum.

Behind etched steel doors was the large and dramatic auditorium. Black velvet covered the walls, relieved by streaks of gold, silver, and flame-shaded terra-cotta. All of the illumination was indirect; the lights were hidden in coves in the proscenium and ceiling. Controlled from a console directly behind the orchestra pit, the lights colored the auditorium in combinations of green, blue, red, and white. The thick carpets were in three tones of green; the seats were in shades of coral. The innovations continued backstage. Most theatres had a lounge, or "Green Room," for leading players. Carroll

ABOVE : The new theatre's streamlined ticket counter. (TH)

212

ABOVE : Orchestra floor, 1931. Each seat had its own program light. (NYHS)

ABOVE : Balcony, 1931. (NYHS)

built an "Orchid Room" for his real stars, the chorus girls. There were club rooms for the crew, practice rooms and a rehearsal hall, publicity offices, a mirror room for last minute costume checks, a pressing room, and even a soundproof broadcasting studio. In the seven stories above the stage forty-four dressing rooms accommodated 130 principals, while the rooms beneath the stage had space for a chorus of 50. And, as was noted in the opening night program, the stage door was guarded not by a doorman but "by girl receptionists as sweet and beautiful as those within the stage confines."

Broadway's second Earl Carroll Theatre opened on 27 August 1931 with the ninth edition of the *Vanities.* Reaction to the building was best summed up by drama critic Brooks Atkinson, who wrote, "Being the theatre's most famous votary of the bizarre and spectacular, Earl Carroll now has a playhouse to match his taste." The public turned out to see the show and its surroundings, but not in sufficient numbers to meet the Carroll's huge weekly expenses of $65,000. A lawsuit to collect unpaid construction costs and the subsequent bankruptcy of investor Edrington left the producer with only one choice. Just six months after it opened Carroll lost his showplace in foreclosure and was forced to continue the *Vanities* at another theatre. Ziegfeld took over the theatre, removed all references to Carroll from its facade, renamed it the Casino, and mounted a hit revival of *Show Boat* starring Paul Robeson. But in the summer of 1932 Ziegfeld died, and once again the theatre changed hands. Its weekly expenses proved to be beyond the means of its final two tenants, however, and both *George White's Music Hall Varieties of 1933* and Sigmund Romberg's last show,

Melody, failed. In 1933, less than two years after it opened, the Earl Carroll Theatre permanently vanished from the legitimate scene.

For the next six years, however, the building still offered entertainment. After a brief fling with movies, the Carroll was converted into a cabaret complete with kitchen, dining tables, and dance floor. As the French Casino it was one of the more successful of the nightclubs that opened in theatres during the thirties. In 1936 Billy Rose took over and rechristened it the Casa Manana. But within three

ABOVE : In 1934 the auditorium was rebuilt into the French Casino, a nightclub. (LC)

years Rose turned his attention to his Aquacade at the 1939 World's Fair and a "for lease" sign went up in the theatre's lobby. This time, though, there were no takers and the Carroll was closed for good. The dressing rooms were sealed, the stage opening bricked up, and the lounges, lobbies, balcony, and most of the auditorium demolished. False ceilings were hung and cinder block walls built in the vast empty spaces of the gutted theatre. Soon the structure reopened as retail space, the remnants of its glamorous past hidden and ultimately forgotten.

Fifty years later, above what had been the stage door, the plaque that read "Through these portals pass the most beautiful girls in the world" has been replaced by a sign welcoming shoppers to Woolworth's. Looking from Seventh Avenue, it's difficult to imagine that this building had ever been a theatre. But from Fiftieth Street that possibility seems less remote. The decorative pattern of ivory, buff, and black brick is clearly visible around the eight flights of darkened dressing room windows.

Inside, it's business as usual at Woolworth's until one reaches the bolted, rusting door of a third-floor storeroom. Unlock it and climb the metal stairs, each step layered with dust and paint chips. The elevator doors are open, but

BELOW : Earl Carroll Theatre exterior, 1990. (NYHS)

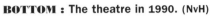
LEFT : Backstage rehearsal hall, 1988. (JP)

BELOW : Outside the dressing room, 1988. (JP)

BOTTOM : The theatre in 1990. (NvH)

the shaft is filled with debris. Without fixtures or furniture the dressing rooms are cold and empty, yet shower tiles and gold-painted window valances still shine as they did when opening-night telegrams and newspaper clippings were tacked to the walls and stuck to the mirrors. Up a ladder and through a trap door in the ceiling of the storeroom, one discovers the remains of the auditorium. Out of the darkness, gold curves and silver pillars, red stripes and torn fragments of soft black velvet become visible. Seemingly suspended from the ceiling, the old proscenium sits high above, a ghostly reminder of the stars and showgirls who passed under it in better times. In 1990, with its businesses evicted and its shops closed, the demolition of the Earl Carroll Theatre, which had begun so many years ago, was finally completed.

ABOVE RIGHT : In 1988 the remains of the old proscenium were discovered above the false ceiling of Woolworth's storeroom. (JP)

BELOW RIGHT : Ceiling and right side wall, 1988. An intact triangular light fixture and remnants of the original black velvet wall coverings are visible. (JP)

ABOVE : Rear auditorium, 1988. Wall markings show where the balcony had been. (JP)

ABOVE : One of the star dressing rooms in 1988. (JP)

EdythTotten
THEATRE
DRAMA · COMEDY

FRENCH HAND
LAUNDRY

TOTTEN THEATRE
THE LIDO GIRL
w EDWARD ELSNER

NATURAL BLOU
CIGAR

C. COHEN
TAILOR

EDYTH TOTTEN THEATRE

247 West 48th Street Paul C. Hunter, 1926

In the time prior to America's involvement in the first world war Broadway's tiniest theatres—the Princess, Little, and Punch & Judy—had enjoyed some popularity with audiences. But when actress Edyth Totten opened the district's fourth petite playhouse in 1926 times had changed. The novelty of intimate theatres had diminished as the cost of running them escalated. Without the hit show that eluded it for thirty years, the Totten's role in the history of Times Square was small. A drama called *Secret Sands* was Totten's first attempt to fill her theatre's 299 seats, but its closing took place soon after its 6 October 1926 premiere. A series of flops followed, and after the sixth (1928's *The Lido Girl*) Totten and her investors were bankrupt. When Preston Sturges' comedy *The Guinea Pig* began its 69-performance run in 1929 the house had been renamed the President, presumably in connection with the Hotel President across the street. Over the years, the Totten changed names and policies a dozen times in attempts to capture the public's interest. German movies took over in 1932, an occasion for which the theatre was dubbed the Hindenburg. By 1933 Germany was out and Italy was in, so the house became the Caruso cinema. On Christmas Day of that year it was renamed the Midget Theatre for the return of live drama. For a few weeks the small showplace was Broadway's only home for all-midget productions. More changes followed. Back to the President in early 1934, then to a three-year stint as the Artef that fall. (The Artef Players was a group of amateur performers who staged many well-received works in the thirties and early forties.) The name on the marquee was Acme Theatre when movies returned in 1937, American Show Shop for legitimate later in 1937, and simply Show Shop for movies in 1938. When the older, larger, and more established 48th Street Theatre down the block was renamed the Windsor its tiny neighbor to the west took over the name, only to give it up shortly after the bigger house reclaimed it in 1943. Once again known as the President, the theatre continued with plays and movies well into the fifties. Its final theatrical use was as Erwin Piscator's Dramatic Workshop. Given the failure that followed the Totten through its various incarnations, it is remarkable that the building survived for so long as a place devoted to the arts. But in 1956 the theatre's luck ended when it was purchased by the adjacent Mamma Leone's. The owners of the restaurant decided that food for the stomach was more important than food for thought and converted the Totten into the expanded eatery's main entrance. The entire structure was demolished in 1988.

LEFT : Edyth Totten Theatre, detail, 1928. (NYHS)

WALDORF THEATRE

116 West 50th Street   Herbert J. Krapp, 1926

Built at a time when new theatres were opening with regularity, the premiere of the Waldorf Theatre in 1926 elicited barely a whisper from the press of the day. While standard generic descriptions like "comfortable" and "attractive" were applied to the theatre, only Alexander Wolcott offered any kind of personal point of view when he claimed the Waldorf was named after "the salad I fancy." Such a modest premiere was in keeping with the subsequent history of the house. Part of the legitimate scene for only six years, the Waldorf ultimately became one of the truly lost Broadway theatres.

Herbert J. Krapp was moonlighting from his job as Shubert house architect when he designed the $1.2 million Waldorf. His plans called for marble wainscoting in the lobby, artifical stone walls in the auditorium, and ornamental plaster panels throughout. Although the house curtain was a large Belgian tapestry, the interior decorations didn't follow any particular period or style, relying instead on colors for effect. As in his other theatres, Krapp eliminated the second balcony for the 1,048-seat Waldorf.   None of the Waldorf's productions was especially memorable, although a few achieved some popularity. The play that began the theatre's brief career had the optimistic title *Sure Thing*. It wasn't, and closed 37 performances after its 20 October 1926 opening. The Waldorf's first hit didn't arrive until its second season. *Take the Air,* a musical starring dancer Will Mahoney, kept the lights on for 204 showings. Between unsuccessful commercial productions, the annual Little Theatre Tournament played the Waldorf in 1929 and 1930. In 1932 a revival of *That's Gratitude* tied the house record of 204 performances. Over the winter, *Whistling in the Dark* chalked up 122 showings and was succeeded by four back-to-back bookings that kept the Waldorf open into the fall of 1933. But despite the busy year, the theatre called it quits after the ninetieth performance of *Dangerous Corner.*   Overshadowed by both the Roxy across the street and Radio City Music Hall down the block, the Waldorf joined its mammoth neighbors in showing movies. The stage and orchestra floor were converted to shops while the balcony was extended towards the screen. But even extra income from stores proved inadequate as the depression deepened, and in 1936 the Waldorf was sold in foreclosure for a fraction of its original cost. The new operators also tried movies, first the domestic variety, then to French imports. Finally, a new gimmick in the field of theatre promotion was introduced. For the cost of a 25-cent admission (plus a handling charge of a dime), everyone attending "Book Nite" at the Waldorf could select a free book from a variety stacked up at the box office. The promotion was discontinued after a few weeks.

In 1941 the remainder of the theatre was converted to retail space. The structure was demolished in the late 1960s to make way for Rockefeller Center's Exxon Building.

JOHN GOLDEN THEATRE

202 WEST 58TH STREET HARRISON G. WISEMAN, 1926

Of the scores of producers, managers, and performers who built themselves a theatre, John Golden was the only one who ever actually built a theatre. At the age of fourteen he was apprenticed to an architectural firm that was constructing a playhouse on 35th Street near Sixth Avenue. If someone passing by the Garrick Theatre should be hit by a falling brick, Golden wrote in his autobiography, it would probably be one he laid.

The stage-struck Golden eventually gave up masonry for an unmemorable acting career, followed by a more successful stint as a lyricist and playwright. The royalties provided enough money to produce his first Broadway show, *Turn To The Right*, which was a huge hit. More winners followed, and by 1923 Golden was the producer of three of the five longest-running shows of the era, including the titleholder, *Lightnin'*. As the profits poured in, Golden decided it was time to have a playhouse of his own. Golden bypassed the congestion of Times Square for a 7,500 square foot plot on 58th Street near Seventh Avenue, directly across the street from the stage door of Jolson's Theatre. He commissioned an 825-seat theatre (leaving the actual construction to others) of the same intimate character as the Booth, Republic, and Gaiety, houses in which his earlier productions had thrived.

The exterior of the new John Golden Theatre was quite plain. Four pairs of doors opened into a narrow lobby. A staircase at the right led to the balcony; additional doors straight ahead gave access to the orchestra. The interior decorations were of a Spanish-Moorish design. The rough-plaster walls were painted beige, embellished with terra-cotta, tones of green, and wrought-iron light fixtures. The seats were upholstered in rich tapestries, and the gold and green house curtain hung below a painting of a Spanish galleon in full sail.

Golden opened his theatre on 1 November 1926 with the transfer from the Little of his production *Two Girls Wanted*. Ten days later, in a rather unexpected move for a producer who just premiered his own playhouse, Golden signed a multi-year lease with the Theatre Guild (whose first home, coincidentally, was the Garrick). The Guild produced the Golden's most famous production in 1928, Eugene O'Neill's *Strange Interlude,* starring Lynn Fontanne. The nine-act, five-hour drama filled every seat for eighteen months.

Many great performers played the Golden, including Edward G. Robinson, Alfred Lunt, Lee Strasberg, Stanford Meisner, and in his stage debut, Paul Muni. Unfortunately, with the exception of *Strange Interlude,* the playhouse had no hits, and Golden lost it in foreclosure during the depression. (He subsequently took over two other theatres—the Royale, which was briefly renamed the Golden, and in 1937 Theatre Masque, which is currently called the Golden.)

Producer John Cort took over the house in 1935 for the staging of intimate musical comedies. Renamed Cort's 58th Street, it opened with *Few Are Chosen*, which sold few tickets.

The theatre's track record and uptown location destined it to join the ranks of playhouses no longer dedicated to the legitimate stage. In the fall of 1936 the house began six successful years as a foreign-film cinema, first as the Filmarte, then as the Fine Arts. The name of the theatre was the Concert when the revue *Of V We Sing* briefly

ABOVE : Proscenium, 1927. (LC)

returned it to the live stage in 1942. The building got religion the next year when it became the headquarters for the Rock Church. The seating capacity was expanded to over 1,000, making plenty of space for all those who wished to participate in "back to the Bible, old-fashioned gospel meetings."

ABOVE : The John Golden Theatre, 1928. (MCNY)

In 1946 the theatre was once again available for legitimate bookings on 58th Street, but the only taker was ABC radio. The network used it as a broadcasting studio for two years, after which it returned to films as the Elysee. When John Golden died in 1955, his first theatre was again in use as a studio for ABC. This time, however, the productions were for television. For the next thirty years the Elysee, which the network called TV-15, was the home for ABC's top game and interview programs, including *The Dick Cavett Show.*

When ABC closed the Elysee in 1985, it was the last remaining old playhouse north of 54th Street. Surrounded by the ghosts of Jolson's and Daly's, the Colonial, Ziegfeld, Majestic, Circle, and New Theatres, the Elysee was doomed to join them. Long forgotten and tucked away too far uptown to attract today's audiences, the theatre passed into the hands of developers without a word from the press or the performers who played there. It was demolished in the fall of 1985.

ABOVE : Exterior view, 1975. (NvH)

ZIEGFELD
RIO RITA
ZIEGFELD
ZIEGFELD
ZIEGFELD PRODUCTION RIO RITA GLORIFYING THE AMERICAN GIRL
MATINEES THURSDAY AND SATURDAY

ZIEGFELD THEATRE

SIXTH AVENUE AT 54TH STREET   THOMAS W. LAMB & JOSEPH URBAN, 1927

By 1926, Florenz Ziegfeld had been glorifying the American girl for two decades. His *Follies* and *Midnight Frolics* were jazzy, flamboyant entertainments perfectly in sync with the optimism of the age. Most of his shows were hits, making fortunes for his stars and backers and spawning imitations like *Earl Carroll's Vanities* and *George White's Scandals.* But the high rollers preferred the real thing; when Ziegfeld made public his desire to build a perfect theatre for stage musicals, William Randolph Hearst and Arthur Brisbane raised the necessary $2.5 million. With the financing in place, Ziegfeld brought together theatre architect Thomas Lamb and *Follies* designer Joseph Urban. The showplace they created was one of the most breathtaking, beautiful buildings ever dedicated to the performing arts. Urban's influence on the design of the Ziegfeld Theatre was unmistakable. In his native Europe he had built bridges for Russian Czars and castles for Hungarian noblemen. In America his sets dazzled fans of the *Follies.* And in New York, his theatre overwhelmed the senses and delighted the critics, including one at *The Architectural Forum,* who did not hesitate to describe this magnificent new addition to Broadway:

> " Considered from without, the playhouse is unlike any other in New York. The facade clearly expresses the purpose of the building. The auditorium is indicated by the bow on the avenue side, and the stage is represented by the ornamentation of the false proscenium. Two large masks, the conventional dramatic symbols of comedy and tragedy, are used at the sides of this proscenium opening. Thus the intent of the building is apparent to the passerby, marking the structure clearly as a temple devoted exclusively to the drama. "

Within, the Ziegfeld also broke architectural conventions. The standard fan-shaped layout was replaced by a unique egg-shaped design, a near perfect ellipse with the stage opening placed at the narrow end. The curves of the auditorium eliminated all corners, providing excellent sightlines and acoustics. The inside of the "egg" was smooth; the single mural decorating it was the largest oil painting in the world.

On the eve of the 2 February 1927 premiere, *The New York Times* published a lengthy description of the Ziegfeld.

> " The decorations, walls, and ceilings are specially designed to tune the mood of the audience to the gay, youthful, and beautiful scenes which the stage unfolds. One enters what seems a hall of gold, the richness of the golden curtain, proscenium, carpets, chairs, lights, affording a setting of ineffable luxury. As the eye wanders from the stage to the walls and ceilings there is a blend from the stark rich gold of the stage to a mural painting of gold, delicately blended with pastel shades of blue and green, which at first seem splashed all over the walls and ceilings like a cubist version of anything at all, but finally take shape in quaint lovely figures like those on a Gobelin tapestry.
> What does this all mean? one asks Mr. Urban. Why, nothing at all. He composed these gay figures of young lovers, some kissing, some running and dancing,

LEFT : Ziegfeld Theatre, northwest corner
of Sixth Avenue and 54th Street, 1927. (LC)

227

ABOVE : Orchestra promenade, 1927. (LC)

some hunting, simply to go with the stage settings. A question of atmosphere. The idea is to throw the audience into the spirit of the thing. **99**

The initial two offerings at the Ziegfeld were hits. The first, a routine musical called *Rio Rita,* managed to entertain audiences for most of the year. The second production, *Show Boat,* made history. "Ol' Man River," "You Are Love," and the rest of Jerome Kern's classic score, with lyrics by Oscar Hammerstein II, were heard for the first time in the Ziegfeld.

After *Show Boat* came more musicals and stars. *Smiles,* Noel Coward's *Bittersweet,* Gershwin's *Show Girl,* Fred Astaire, Bert Lahr, Eddie Foy, Jr., Buddy Rogers, Ruby Keeler, Jimmy Durante, Bob Hope, and Duke Ellington helped make the Ziegfeld one of New York's top musical theatres. (It also had the city's top ticket price on opening nights, an exhorbitant $27.50! Following the premiere of *Ziegfeld Follies of 1931,* Eddie Cantor was seen leaving the theatre with his pried-loose seat in his hands. "For the price I paid," he said, "I deserve to have it.")

After the run of *Hot-Cha!,* Ziegfeld became ill and died in July 1932. Six months later, Hearst took possession of the now closed theatre. Unwilling to finance its operation as a legitimate house, he leased the Ziegfeld to Loew's. The 500-pound brass auditorium doors were replaced by curtains, a screen was hung, and the theatre began ten years of presenting second-run films with a tri-weekly change of program.

The Ziegfeld would have remained a movie theatre had producer Billy Rose not purchased it in 1943; his winning bid of $630,000 cash beat Loew's bid by nearly one hundred thousand dollars. Rose spent an additional quarter of a million to restore all the original structural and decorative details. Once again the Ziegfeld became a "house of hits," presenting *Gentlemen Prefer Blondes, Brigadoon,* a *Porgy and Bess* revival, and *Kismet.*

In 1955 Rose leased the Ziegfeld to NBC. For a period of seven years the network used the theatre for some of its most popular programs, including *The Arthur Mur-*

ABOVE : Auditorium, side view, 1927. (TH)

ABOVE : This striking lounge was under the Ziegfeld's balcony. The large windows to the right face Sixth Avenue. (LC)

ray Dance Party and *The Perry Como Show.* Upon the expiration of the lease NBC restored the theatre to its original condition, and Rose once again made it available for shows. The Ziegfeld only attracted a few bookings during the early sixties. The limited engagements of Maurice Chevalier, Jack Benny, and Danny Kaye were successful, but Bert Lahr's return in *Foxy* and Lillian Gish in *Anya* were not. Without a hit, the costs of maintaining the theatre were proving too much for Rose; property values along Sixth Avenue had skyrocketed and the resulting real estate tax was a "bone-crushing expense for a one-purpose building to carry." Even before *Anya* opened and closed in November of 1965, Rose had purchased the apartment houses and parking lots adjacent to the Ziegfeld, creating the last site on Sixth Avenue with sufficient space for construction of a high-rise office building. The fate of the Ziegfeld was sealed. **B**efore the site could be cleared, however, Rose died. It was now up to his executors to sell the properties to a developer. A deal totaling $17.1 million was made with the Fisher Brothers in the summer of 1966. That September, following a last minute effort to save it by theatre preservationists, the Ziegfeld Theatre was demolished.

During the razing, wrecking crews uncovered a copper box that had been placed in the theatre's cornerstone by Ziegfeld's daughters in 1926. The programs and photographs it contained went to the Lincoln Center library. The statues from the theatre's facade went to the developers, and the house curtain went to the Kennebunkport Country Playhouse in Maine. The Burlington Building went up on the site, and behind it Loew's built a modern movie theatre. They named it the Ziegfeld.

ABOVE : Auditorium ceiling and chandelier, 1927. (LC)

BELOW: Ziegfeld balcony, 1927. (LC)

BELOW : Ziegfeld auditorium, 1927. (LC)

ABOVE : A floor show during the Gallo's days as the Casino de Paris, 1933. (LC)

GALLO OPERA HOUSE

254 WEST 54TH STREET EUGENE DE ROSA, 1927

Broadway theatre, even when it's economically produced and reasonably priced, has always been a risky business. Change the fare to opera and the risk becomes greater. Oscar Hammerstein discovered this with his Manhattan Opera House; so did the leasees of the Century Opera House. Fortune Gallo, the impresario of the San Carlo Opera Company, built a theatre that could house a variety of productions outside his company's season. Never could he have imagined, however, exactly how wide that variety would be.

The nondescript entrance to the Gallo Opera House was located on the ground floor of an equally nondescript sixteen-story office building. The exterior, though, was the only thing ordinary about the Gallo. Past the glass doors of the entrance foyer loomed a magnificent marble lobby nearly one hundred feet long. Lined with mirrored archways and illuminated by crystal chandeliers hanging from its vaulted ceiling, the lobby provided an elegant promenade for the patrons of the opera.

The auditorium itself bordered 53rd Street, and was decorated in the style of the Italian Renaissance. Gold and rose highlighted the bronze-brown walls of the auditorium and accented the dull blue cameo panels that framed the proscenium arch. Five aisles divided the orchestra into four sections; the single upper level was split into a mezzanine and a balcony. Under the recessed sunburst design of the ceiling, over twelve-hundred seats offered an unobstructed view of the stage. In the spacious lounge beneath the main floor, Gallo planned to exhibit souvenirs tracing the history of grand opera in America.

Gallo's company opened his theatre in November 1927 with *La Boheme,* the first production of their unsuccessful three-week season. Once it became apparent that opera would not pay the mortgage, Gallo immediately turned to legitimate shows. The first was Sophocles' tragedy *Electra,* featuring Antoinette Perry. It was withdrawn after twelve performances. *Juno & The Paycock* stayed for five weeks before Gallo leased his theatre to musical comedy producer Phillip Goodman. His first production at the house was *Rainbow,* by Vincent Youmans and Oscar Hammerstein II. Starring Charlie Ruggles and Brian Donlevy, the show was critically admired but was unable to find an audience. It closed a gigantic failure after only 21 performances. The loss was great enough for Goodwin to cancel his lease and abandon the Gallo, which was rapidly earning a reputation as a hard-luck house.

Six weeks after the crash of '29, the theatre was sold in foreclosure for $1,045,000. By January Gallo had left the turbulence of Broadway for the relative calm of his opera company. His playhouse, however, remained part of the legitimate scene a little while longer. Renamed the New Yorker, it presented the 1930 premiere of Ibsen's *The Vikings,* a one-week failure.

Over the next two years eight more flops played the New Yorker, averaging twenty performances apiece. Following the single showing of *Hummin' Sam* in 1933, the theatre was virtually unbookable.

ABOVE : Interior, 1927. (AB)

In 1933 Continental Music Halls, Inc. took over the house and converted it into an elaborate nightclub-restaurant called the Casino de Paris. The seats were replaced with tables that could accommodate 1,100 diners eating meals prepared in a basement kitchen. Drinks could be ordered from The Nudist Bar, its name derived from the explicit paintings surrounding it. Two additional cafes were located in the orchestra and mezzanine, where there also was located a barber shop and beauty salon for last minute touch-ups. Like the Music Hall operating in the adjacent Hammerstein's Theatre, the Casino was run by showman Billy Rose. At his clubs, entertainment was unmatched. A chorus of scantily-clad beauties paraded on a rebuilt stage that extended into the audience. Two orchestras played dance music between shows that featured the likes of Milton Berle, Bill "Bojangles" Robinson, and vaudeville stars Smith & Dale. The Casino de Paris even had house gigolos, who were paid to dance with female patrons who had no partners. Known along Broadway as the "Green Carnation Boys," they were instantly recognizable in the crowded nightclub by the flowers on their lapels. In the frenzy of post-repeal New York, the Casino de Paris outgrossed every legitimate attraction in town. Its success, however, lasted only a brief time. Plagued by labor disputes and battles with the owners, Rose quit the house in 1934. The nightclub closed the following year.

The Palladium was the theatre's name when it reopened in 1936 as an English music hall. Although this incarnation lasted all of three weeks, it did manage to generate the most amusing robbery of the year. Seven days *after* the Palladium closed, a gunman entered the theatre's offices and demanded the previous weekend's receipts from the switchboard operator. Unable to find any cash, the thief instead found a stack of chorus girl photos. He flipped through the pile, removed a shot he liked, put it in his coat pocket, and left. The name of the lucky girl has been lost to history.

The WPA took over the restored house in 1937, renamed it the Federal Music Theatre, and presented a series of concerts and short-lived musicals. The

BELOW : Interior, 1927. (AB)

ABOVE : CBS controlled the Gallo from 1942 until 1976. Over the years, broadcasting companies have leased twenty-three Broadway houses. (NvH)

ABOVE : Interior, 1989. (NvH)

theatre was again known as the New Yorker in 1939 when the government-funded WPA presented *The Swing Mikado*, an update of the Gilbert and Sullivan classic. Transferred to the 44th Street Theatre for a commercial run after only eight weeks, *The Swing Mikado* nevertheless was the longest-running show to play the former opera house. It was also its final legitimate booking. In 1941 the first public display of theatre television was held when a boxing match at Madison Square Garden was projected on a 15 x 20 foot screen mounted on the New Yorker's stage. Considered a novelty at the time, television would eventually play a major role in the theatre's history. In 1942 CBS acquired the New Yorker as their latest Times Square studio. With its stage door adjacent to the 53rd Street entrances to Hammerstein's (which CBS leased in 1936), the New Yorker appealed to the network for reasons of size and location. Designated first as Radio Playhouse No. 4, and later as Studio No. 52, the New Yorker would be one of the network's busiest facilities for nearly three decades. CBS celebrated America's bicentennial by selling Studio No. 52 to Steve Rubell and Ian Schrager. A year later they reopened it as the megawatt disco of all time, Studio 54. A tremendous success, it was noted for an exclusive admission policy based on the belief that "anyplace that hard to get into must be worth waiting for." As the crowds on Fifty-fourth Street grew, so did the theatre's receipts, and the temptation to take a little off the top proved irresistible to Rubell and Schrager. Under federal indictment, they pleaded guilty to skimming more than sixty percent of the gross cash receipts during Studio 54's first two years. The pair sold the club in 1980 before going to prison, where each served a term of twenty months. The theatre remained a disco, nightclub, and part-time cabaret throughout most of the decade. In 1989, the original Italian Renaissance motif was restored as the hall became a full-time venue for rock concerts. Today, over sixty years after Fortune Gallo first opened his opera house, the marquee still reads Studio 54.

ABOVE : Hammerstein's Theatre, 1929. (VC)

HAMMERSTEIN'S THEATRE

1697 BROADWAY AT 53RD STREET   HERBERT J. KRAPP, 1927

It took Arthur Hammerstein eight years to build a memorial theatre bearing his father's name. That was twice as long as the name lasted on the marquee. The realization of a Hammerstein Theatre began after the death of Oscar Hammerstein, the impresario credited with bringing show business to Times Square. Arthur, also a producer, approached the Shuberts with the idea of naming their new theatre on 45th Street after his late father. Although they were unable to reach an agreement and the playhouse opened as the Imperial, Hammerstein did present a number of successful musicals there. One of them, *Rose Marie*, enabled him to finance his own theatre. Hammerstein's Temple of Music was the original name planned for the theatre, but when it opened on November 30, 1927 the playhouse was simply called Hammerstein's. Entering the foyer from the Broadway lobby, patrons first came upon a life-sized bronze statue of Oscar Hammerstein himself. Beyond it, the 1,265 seat auditorium rose up like a giant Gothic cathedral. Ten large stained-glass panels illustrative of the operas Hammerstein produced glowed softly on both sides of the auditorium. The vaulted walls climbed to form a large dome over 50 feet in height; in its center a huge plaster and colored glass lantern illuminated the single balcony. Colorful murals painted to resemble intricate mosaic designs covered the ceiling, and urns that resembled baptismal fonts took the place of proscenium boxes. Patrons entered the theatre to the low tones of live organ music. The overall effect was breathtaking, prompting Brooks Atkinson of the *New York Times* to call it "a splendid new theatre. His Gothic theatre breathes a cathedral air. It is good to have a new theatre which may well become an institution." Hammerstein's got off to a promising start. It's first three attractions were popular with audiences, and each made a lasting contribution to the entertainment industry. *Golden Dawn*, the musical that opened the house, marked the professional debut of Cary Grant (then known as Archie Leach). In 1928's *Good Boy*, "boop-boop-a-doop" girl Helen Kane introduced "I Wanna Be Loved By You," and the following year Helen Morgan first performed "Why Was I Born" in *Sweet Adeline*. Arthur Hammerstein's lucky streak ended with the stock market crash. His next show, *Luana*, was a flop, as was his final musical, *Ballyhoo*, which featured W. C. Fields's last appearance on Broadway. Hammerstein, like so many other producers of the era, declared bankruptcy and was forced out of the theatre he fought so hard to build. It had been open for less than four years. Soon the organ, urns, and statue were auctioned off and removed from the theatre. In December, 1936, the *New York Times* reported that George Blumenthal, Oscar Hammerstein's manager, discovered the bronze statue of his late employer in a junk shop on Centre Street. Apparently Arthur Hammerstein's creditors had sold it for scrap. The shop's proprietor gave Blumenthal one month to raise the $300 necessary to purchase the statue and save it from the furnace. Three weeks later the *Times* reported that Blumenthal was failing in his fundraising efforts. Somehow, though, the statue managed to survive. According to William Hammerstein it was offered for sale to his father, Oscar Hammerstein II, in the mid-forties. He declined the offer. The statue did not surface again until the mid-nineties, when a New Hampshire dealer offered it to the theatre's new owners, CBS, for $5 million. Not surprisingly, the network declined.

The producing team of Schwab and Mandel took over the theatre in 1931 and renamed it the Manhattan. The rededication ceremony on August 4th featured a dazzling lineup of Broadway talent. George Gershwin played "I Got Rhythm" and Jerome Kern performed "Ol' Man River." Even the latest craze, radio, was part of the act. Station WEAF broadcast the special performance, which by all accounts was a smash. Unfortunately, it also was to be the only successful event ever staged at the renamed theatre. After eight months and two flops, Schwab and Mandel called it quits. Earl Carroll, who had just lost his own theatre, signed up next, but even he bailed out after five inactive months. In 1933 Billy Rose stepped in to convert the house into one of his mammoth nightclubs. He replaced the orchestra and balcony seats with tables, installed a kitchen, two large bars, and added illuminated glass steps leading to the on-stage dance floor. Typical programs included magicians, comedians, and troupes of performing midgets. It all helped make Billy Rose's Music Hall (and later, after Rose quit, the Manhattan Music Hall) one of the more popular hot spots in post-repeal New York. The theatre's life as a nightclub ended in 1936 when it was restored for legitimate offerings as the Manhattan. Between February and July the Federal Theatre Project sponsored four shows, including T. S. Eliot's *Murder in the Cathedral*. In the fall of 1936, CBS took a long term lease on the theatre, which has served as a broadcasting studio ever since. As Radio Playhouse No. 1 it hosted such programs as *Major Bowes Amateur Hour*. Later, as Television Studio No. 50, it was home to Ed Sullivan's Sunday night variety show for more than two decades. In 1967 the house was renamed The Ed Sullivan Theatre in honor of the man who, from its stage, first introduced American television viewers to Elvis Presley and the Beatles. CBS purchased the theatre in 1993 and extensively renovated and partially restored it as the home for *The Late Show with David Letterman*. Alterations for broadcasting have taken their toll. The damaged stained-glass windows have been stored by CBS and lighting cables run through holes punched in the great dome now hidden behind sound-absorbing panels. Despite these changes, the theatre's interior was designated a city landmark. Arthur Hammerstein's memorial to his father remains an impressive tribute to the man who turned on the lights along the Great White Way.

ABOVE : The stained-glass windows featured scenes from operas produced by Oscar Hammerstein. (LOC)

ABOVE : Hammerstein's foyer with its plush red and gold Czechoslovakian carpet. At left is the statue of Oscar Hammerstein. (TH)

ABOVE : Interior, 1927. (TH)

BELOW : Proscenium view showing portions of the set for the theatre's premiere production, *Golden Dawn.* (TH)

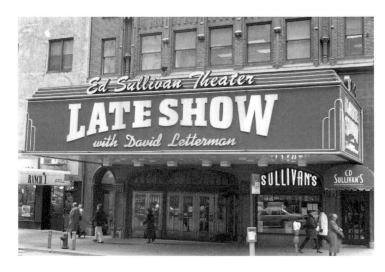

LEFT : Balcony Stairs, 1990. (JP)

ABOVE : Marquee, 1997. An illustration of CBS's 1993 adaptation of the theatre appears on page 281. (NvH)

BELOW : As the Ed Sullivan television studio, 1990. The stage and light grid have been extended over the orchestra, the mosaic ceiling panels obscured by layers of paint, and the stained glass windows hidden behind plywood walls. (JP)

CRAIG THEATRE

152 West 54th Street   R.E. Hall & Company, 1928

The majority of Broadway houses were named after producers, stars, or locations. Even the most generic names like Imperial, Majestic, and Gaiety hinted at the spectacle and pleasures of the entertainments offered on their stages. Such traditions, however, only went so far in the real estate business. Rumor has it that the Craig Theatre was named after the six-year old son of the developer's attorney. Inside and out the Craig was a modest house. The 54th Street entrance lobby extended through the ground floor of a remodeled three-story brownstone to the auditorium on 53rd Street. Seating over 1,400, with a rather large orchestra of 860, the decoration of the single-balcony theatre was quite subdued. The walls were plain plaster, rough in texture and painted autumn brown. Shades of rose, buff, and blue colored the plaster at the back of the house and under the balcony. Wide green fringe bordered the mulberry velvet house curtain. The Gothic arch that outlined the stage opening had no detail except for a simple modeled frame, and the boxes on either side of it were decorated in a Tudor Gothic style. Even before it opened, the Craig was considered an unlucky house. Plagued by construction problems, its 1928 premiere was delayed from Labor Day until Christmas Eve, when first-nighters were treated to the biblical drama *Potiphar's Wife.* Dubbed a "strange little play" by one critic, it ran only two weeks. The next five shows at the Craig were flops, including Preston Sturges' operetta *The Well of Romance* and *Jonica,* an early Moss-Hart collaboration. In 1931, suffering from the effects of the series of failures, an out-of-the-way location, and the depression, the Craig closed. Dark for nearly three and a half years, it reopened in 1934 under new management and a new name, the Adelphi. It's luck, however, was unchanged. When it was rented by the Federal Theatre Project in 1936 it had been open only four weeks out of seventy-two. Two years later the government brought the Adelphi it's first hit. The fifth show in a series of "living newspapers," *...one-third-of-a-nation,* gave 237 performances. When the Theatre Project was dissolved in 1939 the Adelphi again went dark. Unable to attract a legitimate booking, the house was taken over in 1940 by the Royal Fraternity of Master Metaphysicians. Renamed The Radiant Center, it became the home of religious entertainments staged as a labor of love and enlightenment. Union stagehands weren't invited to the party so they picketed the Center, claiming the shows were more song and dance than fire and brimstone. In 1944 the Shuberts put an end to the arguments when they acquired the Adelphi and returned it to true legitimate status. They even managed to come up with a few winners, including *Street Scene, Look Ma, I'm Dancin',* and Leonard Bernstein's impressive debut as a Broadway composer, *On The Town.* The DuMont Television Network signed an eight-year lease in 1949. Among the shows originating from the Adelphi stage was *The Honeymooners,* starring Jackie Gleason and Art Carney.

LEFT : Craig Theatre, 1929. (LC)

ABOVE : Craig auditorium, 1929. (LC)

BELOW : Craig Theatre, 1957. It was renamed the Adelphi in 1934. (SA)

The cameras moved out when the 1957 City Center revival of *Brigadoon* moved in, followed by the final performances of *Damn Yankees*. Renamed the 54th Street in 1958, the theatre continued to host transfers of fading hits, such as *Bye Bye Birdie*, or new ones like *No Strings* and *What Makes Sammy Run?*, waiting for a more desirable theatre. In 1965 the house was renamed again, this time in honor of famed director George Abbott. The musicals that followed could have used his touch. *Darling of the Day,* starring Vincent Price, and *Buck White,* featuring Muhammad Ali in his singing debut, were among the flops. The day Robert Shaw and Rita Moreno began previewing the musical *Gantry* the Hilton chain announced the purchase of the George Abbott Theatre. Acquired from the

Shuberts as the location for a tower addition to their New York Hilton, demolition crews did not have to wait long to clear the site. *Gantry* ran just one performance.

The Craig was the thirty-third new playhouse to open near Times Square in just ten years. Although two others built for film would later convert to live drama, the construction of the Craig signaled an end to the theatre building boom of the twenties. It's demolition forty-two years later was another signal, this time one of the continued shrinking of New York's theatre district.

BELOW : Craig interior, 1929. (LC)

HURLEY Bros & DALY
CENTER Theatre RKO
RKO The CENTER Theatre RKO
The CENTER Theatre
RKO
IDOL OF THE NEW YORK STAGE
ANCIS LEDERER
WITH ELISSA LANDI IN
TWO WORLDS
LEDERER A HIT
ONE-WAY

RKO ROXY THEATRE

6TH AVENUE AND 49TH STREET REINHART & COMPANY, 1932

While the Rockefellers had enough capital to continue with their plans for Rockefeller Center in spite of the depression, they did have the problem of attracting a cash-poor public to their development. The solution to this problem was to include among the towering office buildings two huge theatres, both run by showman extraordinaire S.L. Rothafel, better known as "Roxy." The two "amusement units" of Rockefeller Center were unlike any other in the city. The 6,200-seat Music Hall opened on 27 December 1932 and was devoted to vaudeville and other live entertainment. Two nights later its more "intimate" sister, the 3,700-seat RKO Roxy Theatre, premiered with a stage show and the film *The Animal Kingdom.* Within a few days, however, the Music Hall closed as Rothafel and Rockefeller revamped its policy to duplicate the stage/screen combos at their other theatre across the street. For a time the two theatres complemented each other. Not only did their presentations match, so did their marquees. Both had huge lobbies, lounges, and foyers, and each had three balconies. Their stages could be raised and lowered in sections or revolve as one giant turntable. The orchestra platforms could travel on or under the stages, both of which were framed by huge contour curtains taking any of two hundred possible shapes. Here the similarities ended. While the Music Hall's auditorium was (and still is) a gilded art deco sunburst with cove lighting effects, the RKO Roxy presented a less dramatic appearance. The seventy-foot high walls were paneled in rich mahogany and supported a flat ceiling decorated with figures from Greek mythology. Centered over the orchestra was a six-ton, 104,000-watt chandelier thirty-feet in diameter. Said to have been the largest of its kind ever built, the fixture required its own fan cooling system. Downstairs, the two-thousand square foot Grand Lounge featured furniture upholstered in red leather. In the men's lounge was a photo mural depicting the history of aviation; in the women's, a mural entitled "Amelia Earhart Crossing the Atlantic." The most startling difference between the two theatres, however, was found at the box office. The Music Hall's new policy was a smash, causing business at the RKO Roxy to suffer from the competition. The smaller theatre's problems were compounded by a lawsuit from the owners of the Roxy Theatre, a five-year old movie palace also built for Rothafel. They successfully challenged Rothafel's right to use his own nickname on a theatre marquee, and after much litagation, forced its removal in 1933. The name of the house was changed to the RKO Center Theatre, and the features changed from first-run movies to less expensive second-run double-bills. The RKO Center was operated as a movie theatre until July 1934, when the "RKO" was dropped as the house closed in preparation for its first legitimate booking, the Strauss operetta *The Great Waltz.* Featuring 200 performers and 55 musicians among crystal chandeliers and lit candelabra, the show used the turntable and elevators of the stage to create breathtaking scene changes. After nine months the show left New York on tour, leaving the Center to once again meet its expenses by showing movies.

LEFT : RKO Roxy Theatre in 1934, about six
months after being renamed the Center. (NYHS)

ABOVE : RKO Roxy Theatre prior to its 1932 opening. (LC)

Soon it became apparent that the only successful attractions at the Center would be stage extravaganzas. *The White Horse Inn* opened in 1936, offered a Tyrolean village on stage and Tyrolean shops in the lobby, and ran nearly seven months. In 1937 the Rockefellers commissioned *Virginia,* a musical about colonial Williamsburg. (Williamsburg's restoration was a Rockefeller family project.) Audiences prefered Austria to America, and *Virginia* closed after sixty performances. **T**wo more legitimate shows tried to fill the mammoth Center in 1939. *The American Way,* an epic play starring Frederic March, kept the lights on for nine months. But even Louis Armstrong, Benny Goodman, Butterfly McQueen, and Walt Disney-inspired sets couldn't save *Swingin' The Dream.* A jazz version of *A Midsummer Night's Dream,* it was a 13-performance disaster. With its closing, the Rockefellers looked beyond the legitimate theatre for amusements more suited to the giant Center. **T**heir search ended with skating star Sonja Henie, who took over the theatre for *It Happens on Ice* in October 1940. With the stage rebuilt as an ice rink, the spectacle was a tremendous success. It and a subsequent series of ice shows kept the Zamboni parked next to the Center Theatre for ten years. When the ice finally melted in 1950, the Rockefellers leased the Center to the National Broadcasting Company, which used the theatre as a television studio for four years. **I**n 1954, with midtown office space at a premium, the twenty-two year old theatre was demolished. A nineteen-story skyscraper replaced the auditorium without much difficulty. But razing the Center's six-story lobby, which was located in the bottom of another office tower, was not so easy. The lower floors were stripped to the steel supports while the upper stories remained intact, giving the disarming illusion that the skyscraper was being torn down from the bottom up.

ABOVE : RKO Roxy auditorium, 1932. (NYHS)

248

ABOVE : RKO Roxy Theatre grand foyer, 1932. (NYHS)

BILTMORE THEATRE

261 WEST 47TH STREET   HERBERT J. KRAPP, 1925

In the mid-1920s the Chanin brothers, engineers and builders, challenged the Shubert empire by constructing six new playhouses in the heart of the theatre district. The 948-seat Biltmore was their second, destined to be the home of many long-run comedies.

The Biltmore opened with a transfer from Cohan's Theatre, the farce *Easy Come, Easy Go*. Highlights of the theatre's first decade were star turns by Claudette Colbert and James Stewart, but long-run success eluded the Biltmore until director George Abbott and the studio Warner Brothers acquired it in 1936. Five smashes followed over the next fifteen years—the comedies *Brother Rat*, *What a Life*, *My Sister Eileen*, *Kiss and Tell*, and the drama *The Heiress*. In 1951 the two owners sold the theatre for $275,000 to developer Irving Maidman, who promptly leased it to CBS for ten years. The Biltmore became Studio No. 62, the network's sixteenth Manhattan television facility.

CBS moved out in 1961 and the comedy *Take Her, She's Mine* opened for a year's run. The Biltmore's next hit arrived in 1963. Neil Simon's *Barefoot in the Park*, starring Robert Redford, kept Biltmore audiences laughing for over fifteen-hundred performances. The theatre's biggest success, however, came not with a comedy but with a musical that captured the spirit of an entire generation. *Hair* began life off-Broadway at Joseph Papp's New York Shakespeare Festival, but settled into the Biltmore for a record-breaking four years in 1968.

Though many shows opened at the Biltmore in the seventies and eighties, none of them enjoyed a long run. In 1986, David Cogan, who had purchased the theatre from Maidman for $850,000 in 1958, sold it for $5 million to real estate investor Sam Pfeiffer, who hoped to cash in on the value of the theatre's air rights. But in December of 1987, just a month after the Biltmore's interior was designated a landmark, arsonists set fires on the stage and in the auditorium. Later vandals and scavengers broke in, leaving the theatre in such a deteriorated condition that the city declared it unsafe. Meanwhile, Pfeiffer's three attempts to auction the neglected Biltmore failed. Pfeiffer defaulted on his mortgage and the bank took possession of the historical eyesore.

In 1993 James Nederlander and Stewart Lane, partners in the Palace Theatre, bought the Biltmore for $550,000. Four years later, after failing to win wage and staffing concessions from theatre unions, they sold the playhouse to developer Joseph Moinian. The theatre's auditorium is scheduled to be restored and incorporated into a new hotel, but its future as a legitimate playhouse is very much in doubt.

LEFT : Biltmore interior, 1997. Vacant since the musical review *Stardust* closed in 1987, the theatre has been ravaged by fire, vandalism, and neglect. (NvH)

RIGHT : The Biltmore's exterior is similar to that of the 49th Street Theatre (page 206), also designed by Krapp. (NvH)

HOLLYWOOD THEATRE

1655 BROADWAY AND 237 WEST 51ST STREET   THOMAS W. LAMB, 1930

The age of the opulent movie palace was almost over when Warner Brothers built the Hollywood Theatre in 1930. Dedicated as a memorial to the late Sam Warner, the theatre tried to compete with the Capitol, the Paramount, and the Roxy by touting itself as New York's first movie palace designed for talkies. The Hollywood found success as a movie theatre to be elusive. In 1934, as so many live theatres were converting to film, the Hollywood bucked the trend and presented its first stage show, *Calling All Stars*. Warners was undeterred by the revue's short run and the theatre alternated between live shows and films for the next fifteen years. The most memorable production of this period was *Romeo and Juliet* with Laurence Olivier and Vivien Leigh as the ill-fated lovers. It was also during this time that the theatre's Broadway entrance was closed and, during legitimate bookings, its name was changed to the 51st Street Theatre. In 1949 the silver screen was permanently retired when the theatre was renamed for the noted Broadway columnist Mark Hellinger. Eleven shows played the sixteen-hundred-seat Hellinger until the big one arrived in 1956. Lerner and Loewe's *My Fair Lady*, starring Rex Harrison and Julie Andrews, became Broadway's longest-running musical at 2,717 performances and kept the Hellinger lit until 1962. The fortunes of the Hellinger fluctuated over the next three decades. *Jesus Christ Superstar* and *Sugar Babies* were huge hits, *On A Clear Day You Can See Forever* and Katherine Hepburn in *Coco* had respectable runs, but *A Joyful Noise*, *1600 Pennsylvania Avenue*, *Grind*, and *Rags*, among many others, flopped. In 1984 the movie version of *A Chorus Line* used the Hellinger as its primary location and prominently features the theatre in many scenes. After the 1989 demise of yet another big musical, *Legs Diamond*, and with no other bookings on the horizon, the Nederlander Organization leased the Hellinger to the non-denominational Times Square Church for $1 million a year. The church purchased the landmarked building three years later for a reported $17 million, ending the Hellinger's theatrical life for the foreseeable future.

LEFT : The Hollywood's rococo interior is one of the most ornate remaining in Manhattan. Decorated in red, gold, and brown, it is highlighted by a dozen murals depicting the French aristocracy at play. Entered through a stunning three-story rotunda, the well-maintained theatre remains open to the public for church services. (NvH)

RIGHT : Familiar to theatre-goers as the Mark Hellinger, the landmarked musical house became the home of the Times Square Church in 1989. (NvH)

APPENDIX

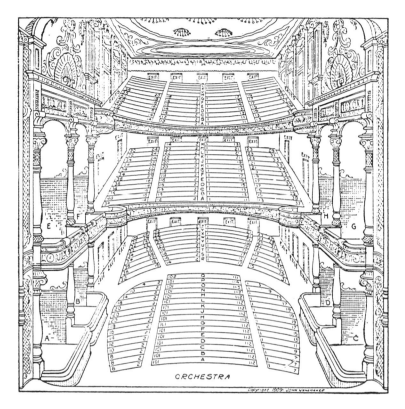

BROADWAY THEATRE : Seating diagram, 1909. (WM)

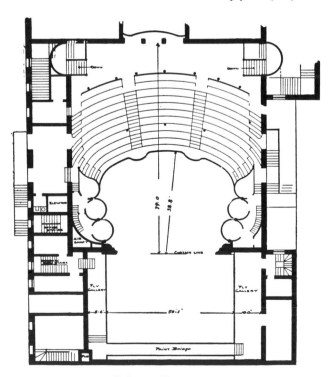

AMERICAN THEATRE : Gallery plan. (WB)

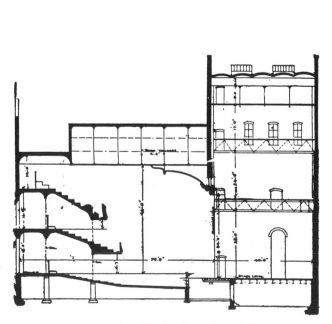

ABBEY'S THEATRE : Longitudinal section. (WB)

EMPIRE THEATRE : Balcony Plan. (WB)

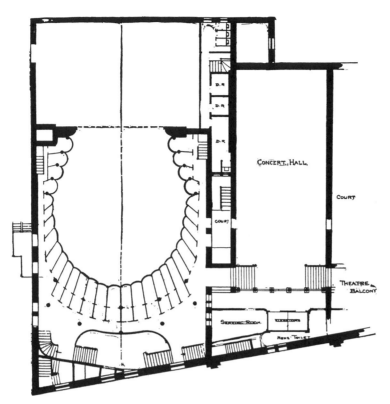

OLYMPIA THEATRE : Balcony plan. Olympia Music Hall is at left. (WB)

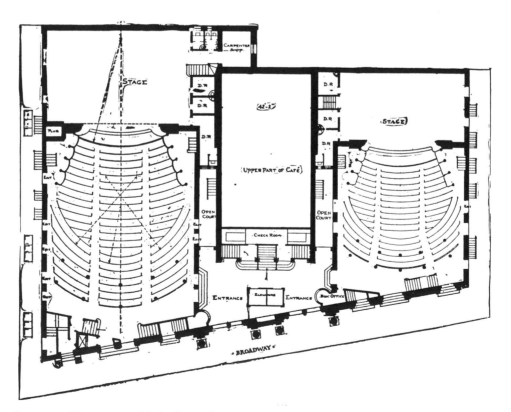

OLYMPIA THEATRE : Main floor plan. (WB)

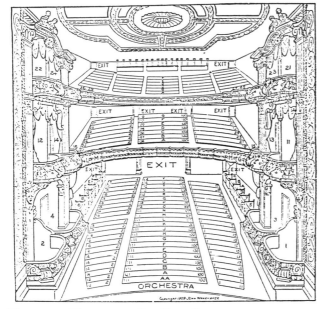

VICTORIA THEATRE : Seating diagram, 1909. (WM)

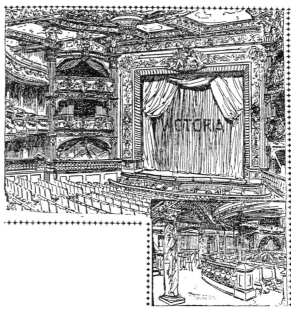

VICTORIA THEATRE : Interior views. (WM)

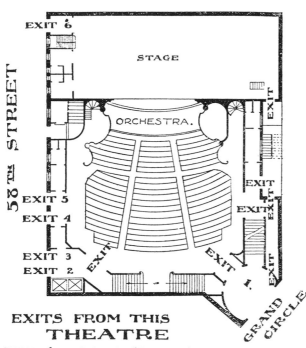

EXITS FROM THIS THEATRE

EXIT : 1 LEADS TO GRAND CIRCLE
Nº 2.3.4.5.6. LEAD TO 58 TH ST.

MAJESTIC THEATRE : Orchestra diagram.

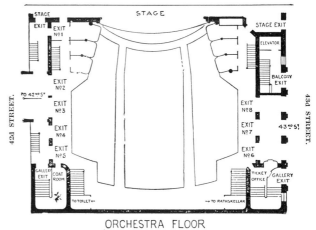

ORCHESTRA FLOOR

EXITS 1, 2, 3, 4, 5 lead to 42d Street; Exits 6, 7, 8 lead to 43d Street.

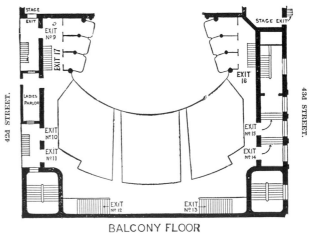

BALCONY FLOOR

EXITS 9, 10, 11, 17 lead to 42d Street; Exits 14, 15, 16 lead to 43d Street;
Exits 12 and 13 lead by staircase to lower floor.

LYRIC THEATRE : Orchestra diagram.

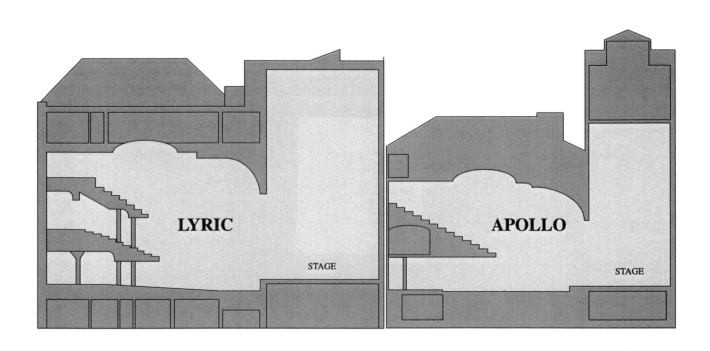

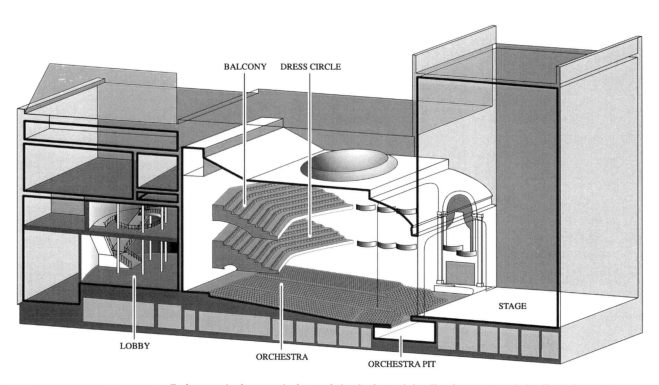

LYRIC AND APOLLO THEATRES : Before and after renderings of the Lyric and Apollo theatres and the Ford Center for the Performing Arts as viewed from 43rd Street. Among the architectural elements reused in the new facility are the Lyric's 43rd Street facade and the Apollo's proscenium and auditorium dome. (BK)

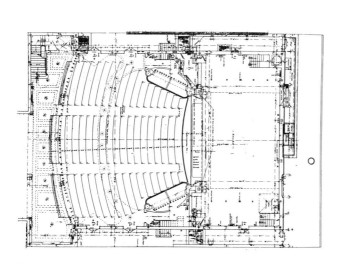

HUDSON THEATRE : Orchestra plan. (AB)

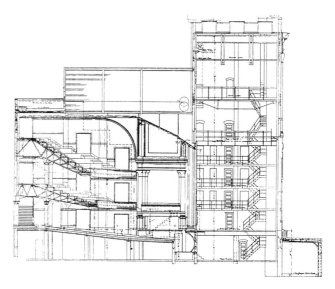

HUDSON THEATRE : Longitudinal section. (AB)

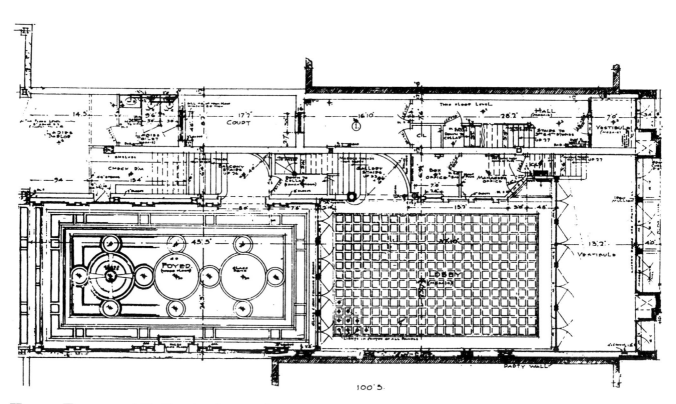

HUDSON THEATRE : 44th Street entrance plan. (AB)

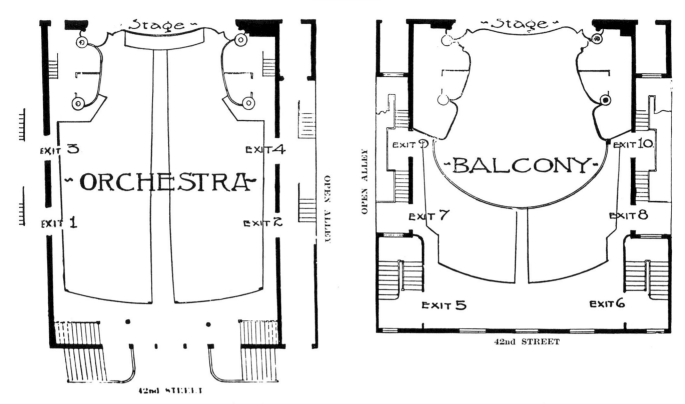

Lew M. Fields Theatre : Orchestra diagram, 1904.

Lew M. Fields Theatre : Balcony diagram, 1904.

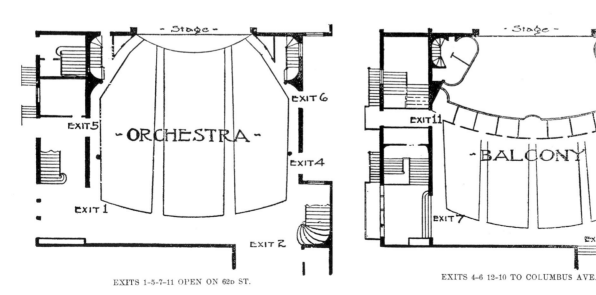

EXITS 1-5-7-11 OPEN ON 62D ST.

EXITS 4-6 12-10 TO COLUMBUS AVE.

Colonial Theatre : Orchestra diagram, 1905.

Colonial theatre : Balcony diagram, 1905.

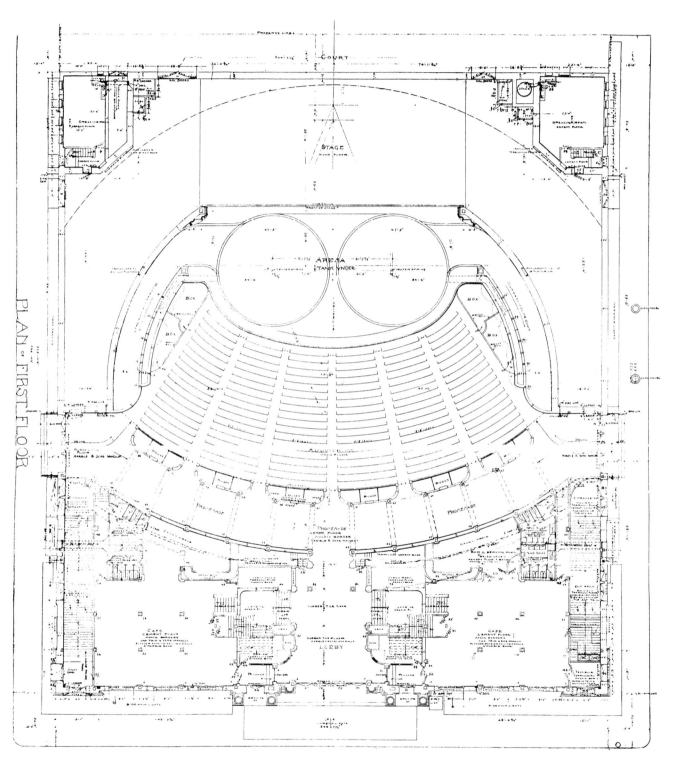

HIPPODROME THEATRE : Main floor and upper gallery plans. (AA)

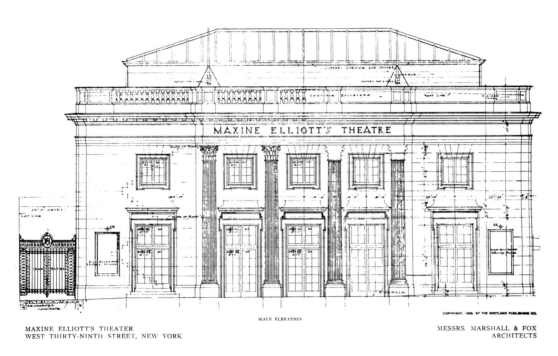

MAXINE ELLIOTT'S THEATER
WEST THIRTY-NINTH STREET, NEW YORK

MESSRS. MARSHALL & FOX
ARCHITECTS

MAXINE ELLIOTT'S THEATRE : Main elevation. (AA)

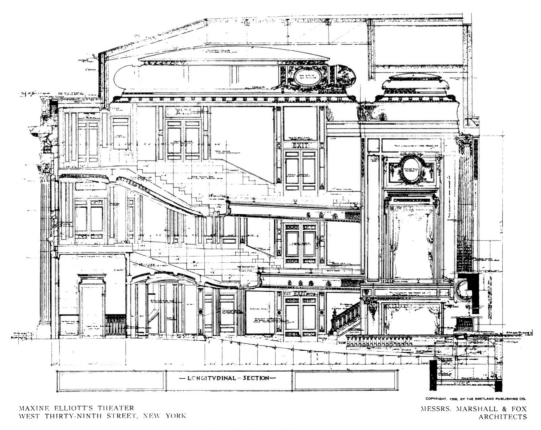

MAXINE ELLIOTT'S THEATER
WEST THIRTY-NINTH STREET, NEW YORK

MESSRS. MARSHALL & FOX
ARCHITECTS

MAXINE ELLIOTT'S THEATRE : Longitudinal section. (AA)

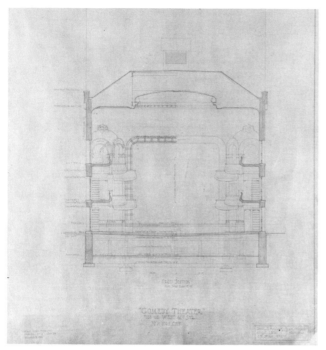

COMEDY THEATRE : Cross section. (SA)

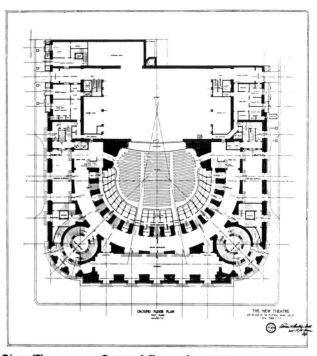

NEW THEATRE : Ground floor plan. (AA)

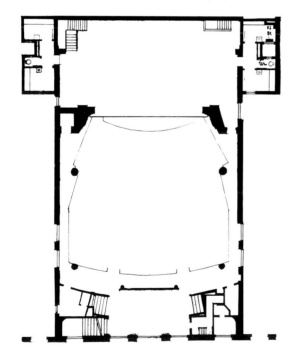

63RD STREET MUSIC HALL : Ground floor diagram. (NvH)

FRONT ELEVATION, THIRTY-NINTH STREET THEATRE, NEW YORK
MR. WILLIAM ALBERT SWASEY, *ARCHITECT*

NAZIMOVA'S THEATRE : Front elevation. (AA)

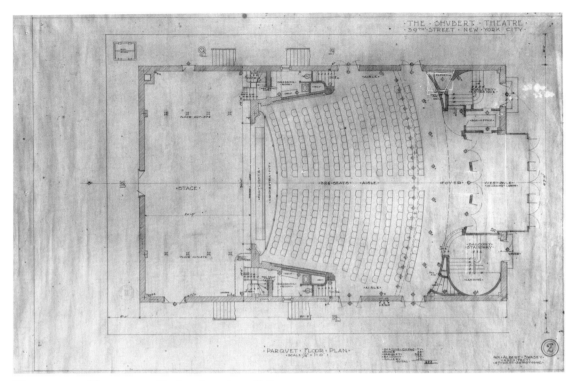

NAZIMOVA'S THEATRE : Orchestra plan. (SA)

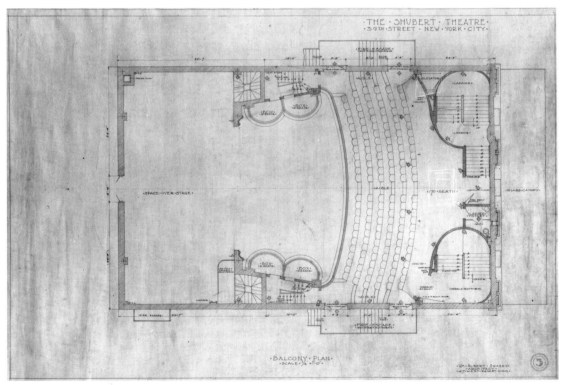

NAZIMOVA'S THEATRE : Balcony plan. (SA)

APPENDIX

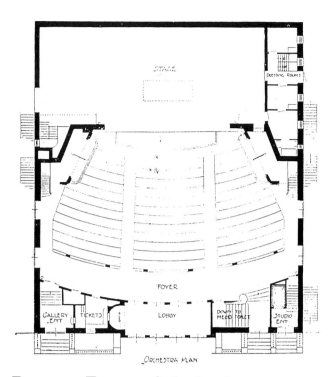

PLAYHOUSE THEATRE : Orchestra plan. (AB)

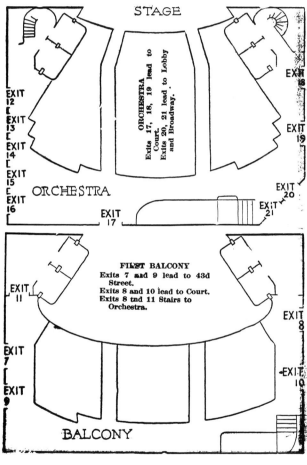

GEORGE M. COHAN THEATRE : Orchestra and balcony diagrams.

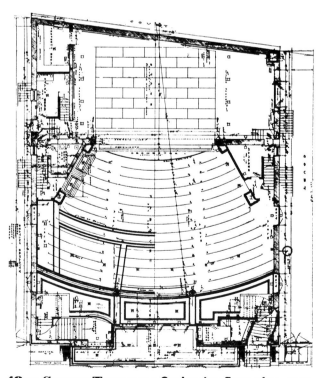

48TH STREET THEATRE : Orchestra floor plan. (AA)

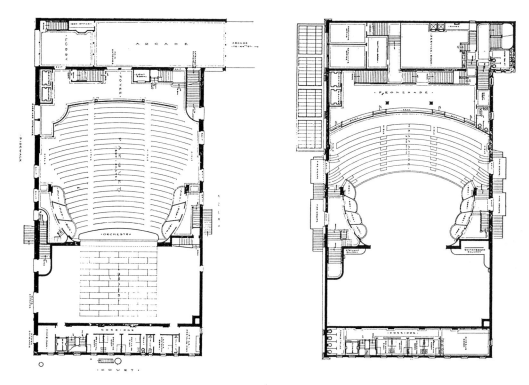

WEBER AND FIELDS' MUSIC HALL : Orchestra and mezzanine plans. (AB)

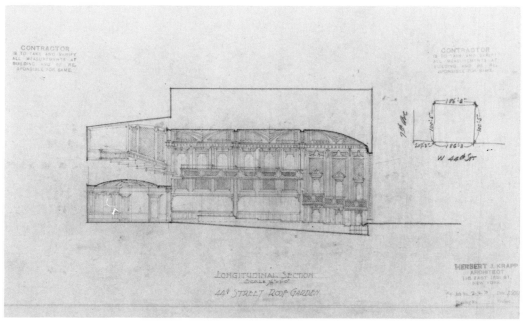

WEBER AND FIELDS' MUSIC HALL : Longitudinal section of the 44th Street Roof Garden, remodeled by Herbert J. Krapp in 1917. (SA)

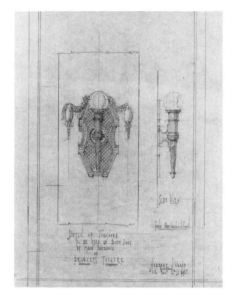

PRINCESS THEATRE : Rendering of exterior light fixture, 1913. (SA)

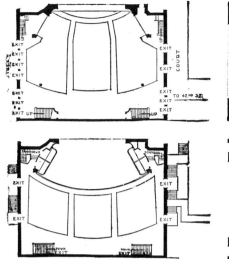

CANDLER THEATRE : Diagrams.

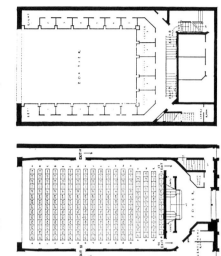

PUNCH AND JUDY THEATRE : Orchestra and box diagrams.

ELTINGE THEATRE : Proposed interior of the AMC Empire 25 Cinema theatre lobby, 1997. The relocated and restored Eltinge Theatre will house the box office, cafe, escalators, and entrances to twenty-five new movie auditoriums. (BTA)

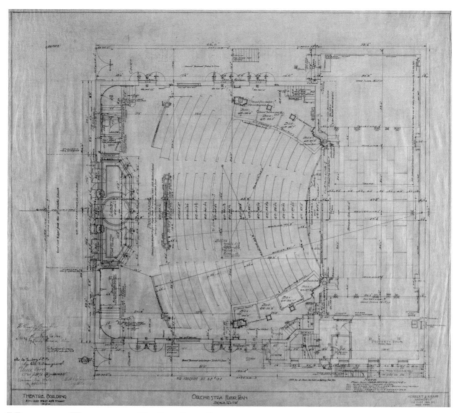

MOROSCO THEATRE : Orchestra plan. (SA)

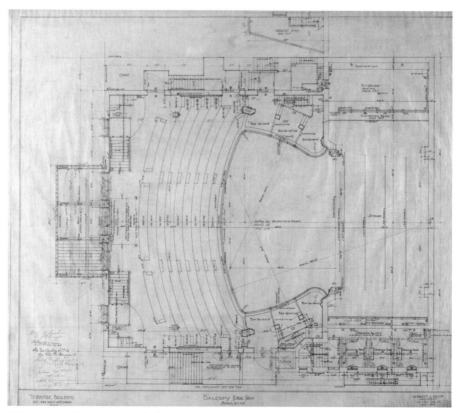

MOROSCO THEATRE : Balcony plan. (SA)

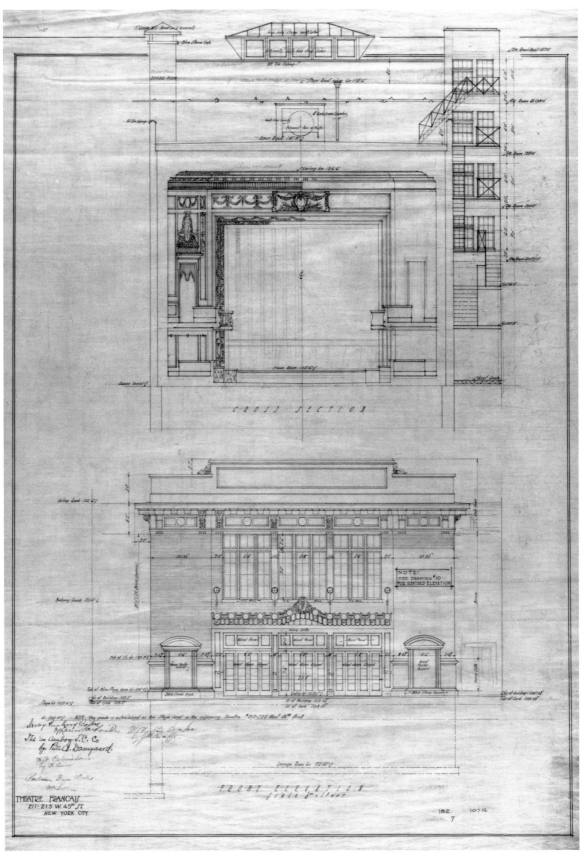

BIJOU THEATRE : Front elevation and cross section. (SA)

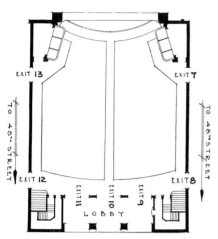

VANDERBILT THEATRE : Orchestra diagram.

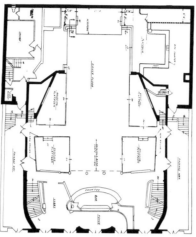

HENRY MILLER'S THEATRE : Ground floor plan as Shout. (NvH)

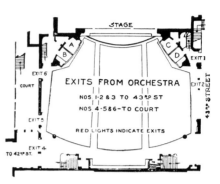

SELWYN THEATRE : Orchestra diagram.

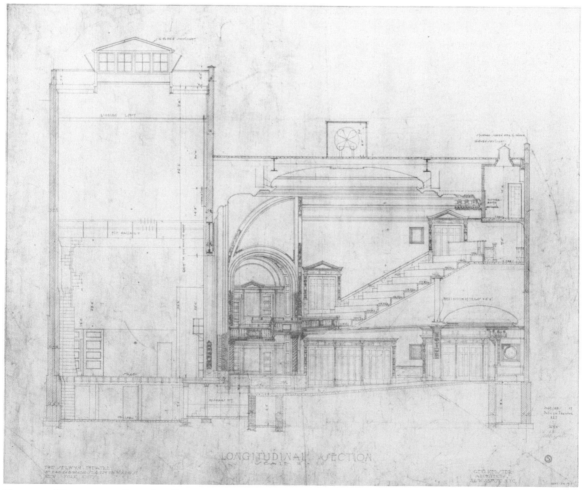

SELWYN THEATRE : Longitudinal section. (SA)

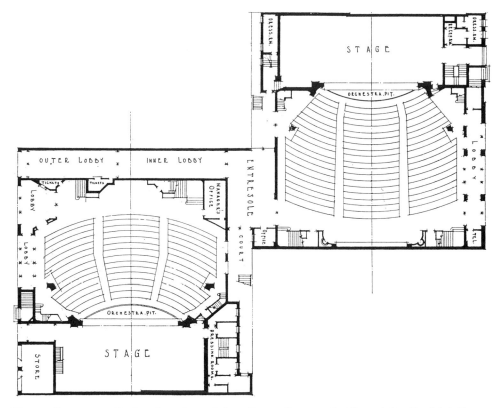

TIMES SQUARE : Orchestra plan of the Times Square (left) and Apollo (right). **(AB)**

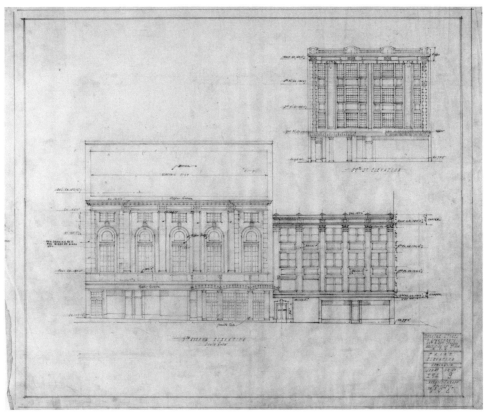

JOLSON'S 59TH STREET THEATRE : Seventh Avenue elevation. **(HK)**

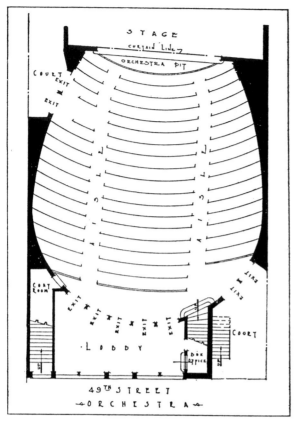

49TH STREET THEATRE : Orchestra diagram.

49TH STREET THEATRE : Balcony diagram.

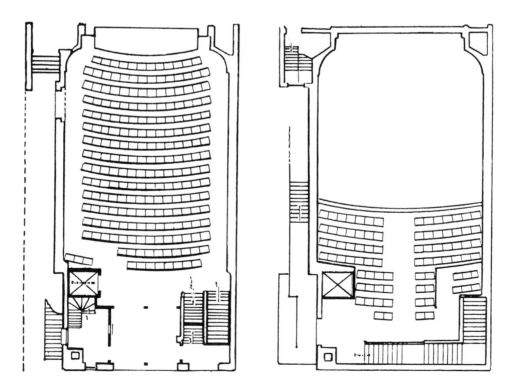

EDYTH TOTTEN THEATRE : Orchestra and balcony diagrams.

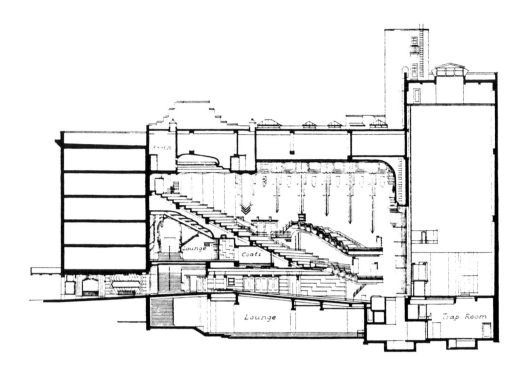

EARL CARROLL THEATRE : Longitudinal section. (AB)

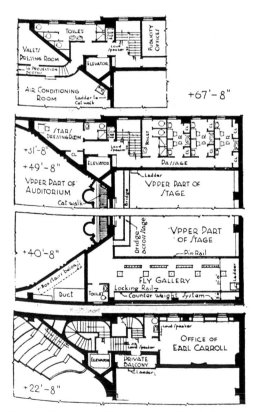

EARL CARROLL THEATRE : Backstage plan detail. (AA)

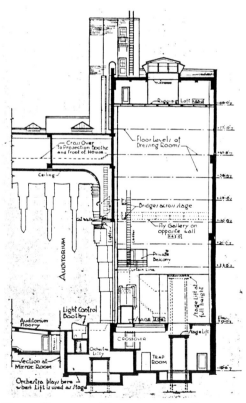

EARL CARROLL THEATRE : Section detail. (AA)

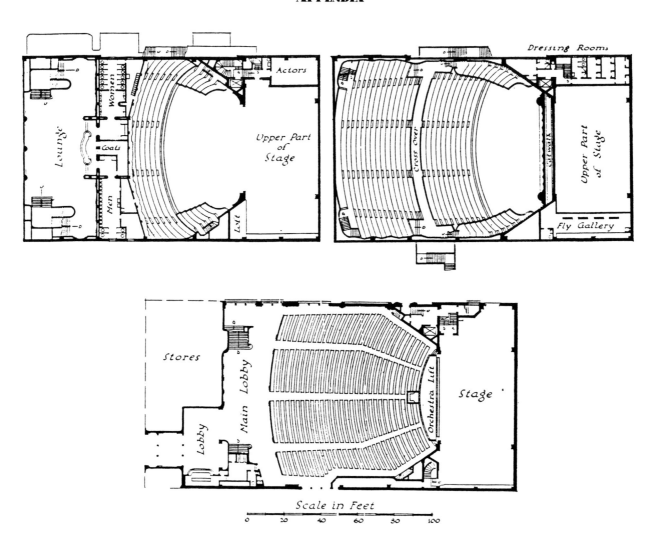

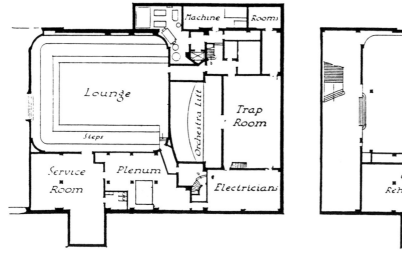

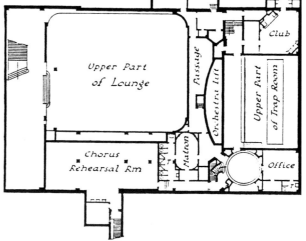

EARL CARROLL THEATRE : Plans, 1931. (AA)

WALDORF THEATRE : Herbert J. Krapp's 1926 rendering of the Waldorf exterior. (HK)

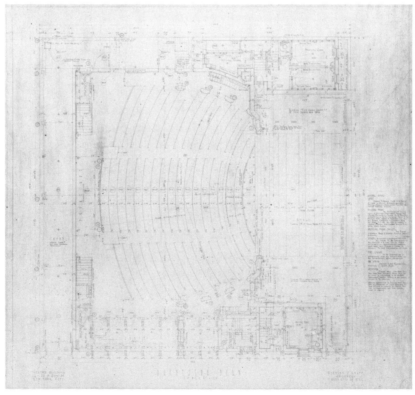

WALDORF THEATRE : Orchestra plan. (SA)

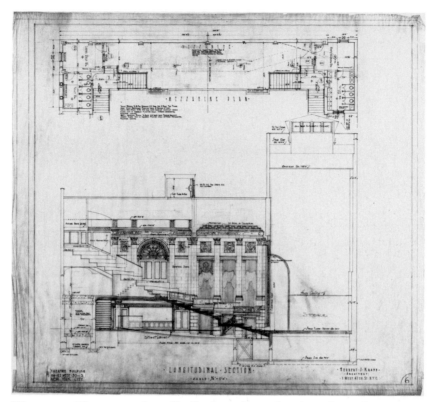

WALDORF THEATRE : Longitudinal section showing alterations as a movie house with retail stores added in the former orchestra and stage areas. (HK)

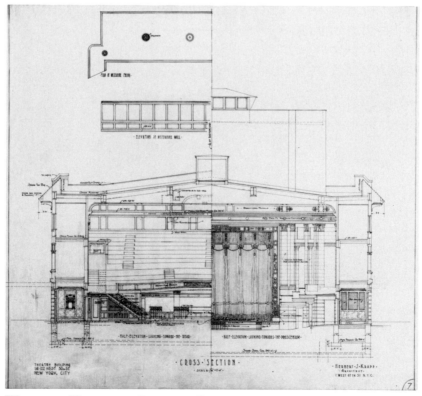

WALDORF THEATRE : Cross section. (HK)

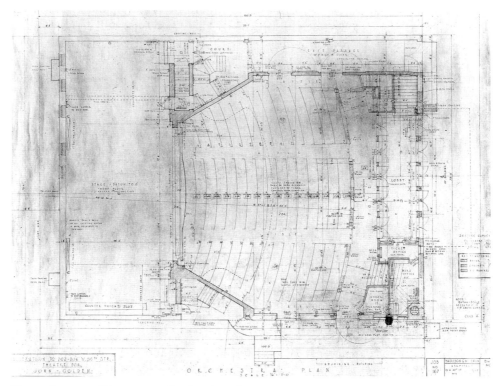

JOHN GOLDEN THEATRE : Orchestra plan. (SA)

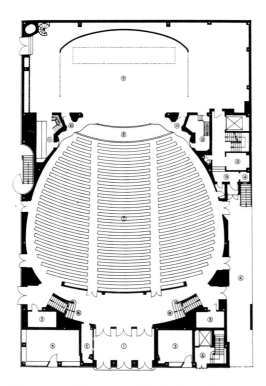

ZIEGFELD THEATRE : Orchestra plan.

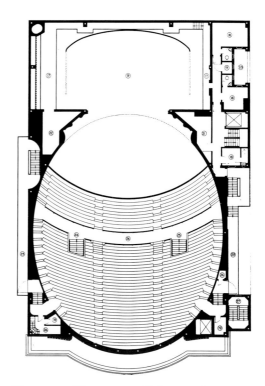

ZIEGFELD THEATRE : Balcony plan. (JU)

ZIEGFELD THEATRE : Joseph Urban's early design for the Ziegfeld Theatre. (LC)

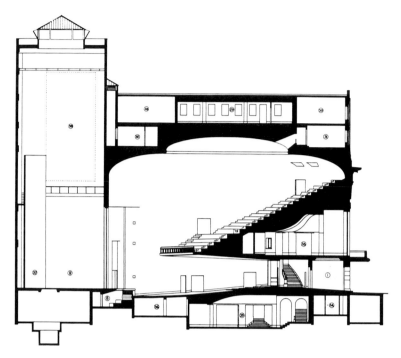

ZIEGFELD THEATRE : Longitudinal section. (JU)

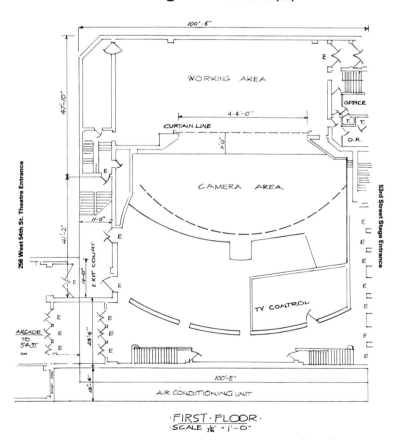

GALLO OPERA HOUSE : Orchestra plan during theatre's use as a television studio. (NvH)

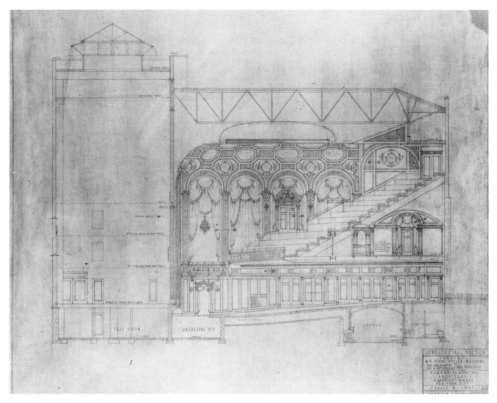

GALLO OPERA HOUSE : Longitudinal section. (SA)

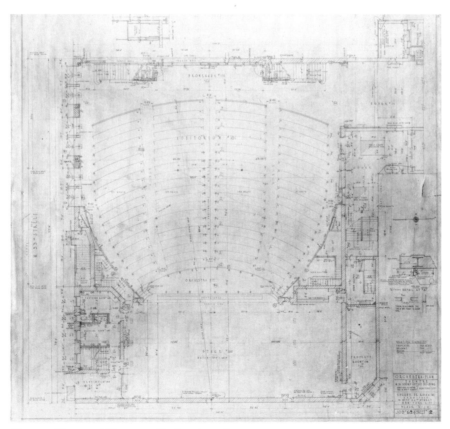

GALLO OPERA HOUSE : Orchestra plan, 1927. (SA)

HAMMERSTEIN'S THEATRE : Longitudinal section. (HK)

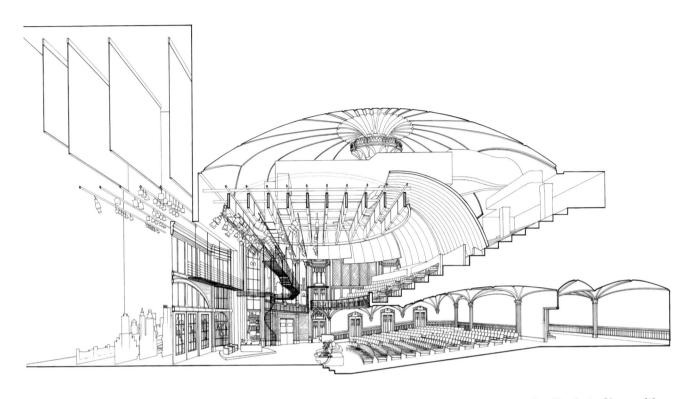

HAMMERSTEIN'S THEATRE : The 1993 adaptation of the Ed Sullivan Theatre by CBS as the set for *The Late Show with David Letterman*. A smaller space was created within the larger auditorium, with accoustical baffles reducing the balcony size and masking the high dome and air-conditioning ducts. (PPA)

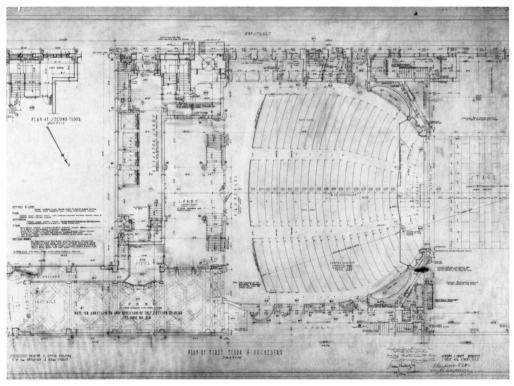

HAMMERSTEIN'S THEATRE : Orchestra plan. (HK)

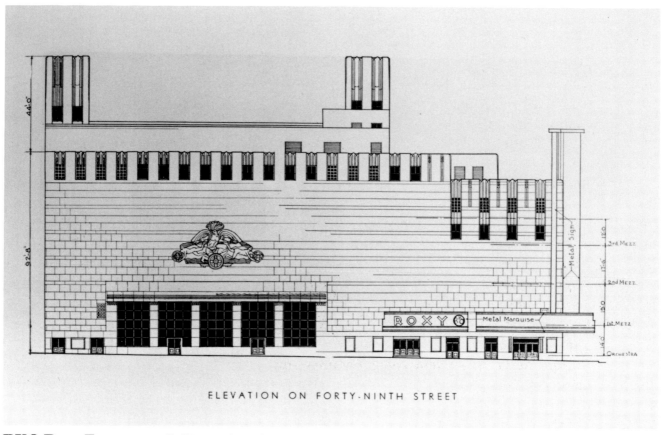

ELEVATION ON FORTY-NINTH STREET

RKO ROXY THEATRE : 49th Street elevation. **(AA)**

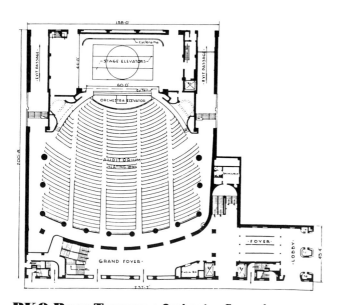

RKO ROXY THEATRE : Orchestra floor plan. **(AA)**

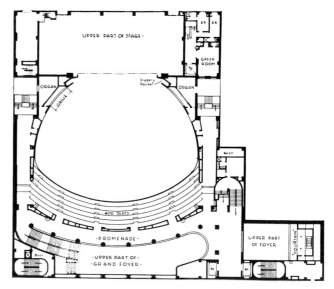

RKO ROXY THEATRE : First mezzanine floor plan.
The second and third mezzanines, seating 655 and
558 respectively, brought the theatre's total
capacity to 3,509. **(AA)**

PHOTO CREDITS

AA	*The American Architect*
AB	*Architect's and Builder's Magazine*
AM	Andrew Moore
BK	Beyer Blinder Belle Architects & Planners, LLP/Kofman Engineering Ltd.
BTA	American Multi-Cinema, Inc. (AMC)/BTA Architects Inc. & Gould Evans Goodman Associates
PL	Detroit Public Library
GMU	Library of Congress Federal Theatre Project Collection, George Mason University
HC	Harvard College Theatre Collection
HK	Herbert J. Krapp Collection
JP	Jock Pottle
JU	Joseph Urban, *Theatres*
LAPL	Security Pacific Historical Photograph Collection—Los Angeles Public Library
LC	The Billy Rose Theatre Collection—The New York Public Library at Lincoln Center; Astor, Lenox and Tilden Foundations
LOC	Library of Congress
LS	Lee Snider
MCNY	Theatre Collection, Museum of the City of New York
MH	Maggie Hopp
NvH	Nicholas van Hoogstraten
NYHS	New York Historical Society
NYPL	New York Public Library
PPA	Polshek and Partners Architects
SA	The Shubert Archives
TH	Terry Helgesen Collection
TM	*Theatre Magazine*
TX	Theatre Arts Collection, Harry Ransom Humanities Research Center, The University of Texas at Austin
VC	Violet Carlson
WB	William Birkmire, *The Planning and Construction of American Theatres*
WC	Whitney Cox
WISC	Wisconsin Center for Film and Television
WM	William Morrison Collection
YL	Old York Library

Uncredited diagrams and plans originally appeared in theatre programs.

BIBLIOGRAPHY

Atkinson, Brooks. *Broadway.* New York: Macmillan, 1970.

Birkmire, William H. *The Planning and Construction of American Theatres.* New York: John Wiley & Sons, 1906.

Bordman, Gerald. *American Musical Theatre.* New York: Oxford University Press, 1978.

Chapman, John, ed. *Best Plays.* New York: Dodd, Mead, and Company, 1947-1952.

Clarke, Norman. *The Mighty Hippodrome* New York: A.S. Barnes and Company, 1968.

Golden, John and Shore, Viola Brothers. *Stagestruck John Golden.* New York: Samuel French, 1930.

Green, Stanley. *Ring Bells! Sing Songs! Broadway Musicals of the 1930's.* New York: Arlington House, 1971.

Guernsey, Otis L., Jr. ed. *Best Plays.* New York: Dodd, Mead, and Company, 1964-1982.

Henderson, Mary C. *The City and the Theatre.* Clifton, New Jersey: James T. White & Company, 1973.

Hewes, Henry, ed. *Best Plays.* New York: Dodd, Mead, and Company, 1961-1964.

Johnson, Stephen Burge. *The Roof Gardens of Broadway Theatres 1883-1942.* Ann Arbor, Michigan: UMI Research Press, 1985.

Kronenberger, Louis, ed. *Best Plays.* New York: Dodd, Mead, and Company, 1952-1961.

Mantle, Burns, ed. *Best Plays.* New York: Dodd, Mead, and Company, 1919-1947.

Mantle, Burns, and Sherwood, Garrison P., eds. *Best Plays.* New York: Dodd, Mead, and Company, 1899-1919.

McGill, Raymond D.,ed. *Notable Names in the American Theatre.* Clifton, New Jersey: James T. White and Company, 1976.

Murray, Ken. *The Body Merchant.* Pasadena, California: Ward Ritchie Press, 1976.

Sheean, Vincent. *Oscar Hammerstein.* New York: Simon and Shuster, 1956.

Stagg, Jerry. *The Brothers Shubert.* New York: Random House, 1968.

Suskin, Steven. *Show Tunes 1905-1985.* New York: Dodd, Mead, and Company, 1986.

Urban, Joseph. *Theatres.* New York: Theatre Arts, Inc., 1929.

Young, William C. *Documents of American Theatre History.* Chicago, Illinois: American Library Association, 1973.

Credit is also due the hundreds of anonymous reporters and columnists who were the sources of the facts and stories included in each chapter. Their articles appeared in the following publications:

American Architect (1885, 1905, 1909, 1922, 1923, 1927, 1930, 1932)
Architectural Forum (1927, 1931-1933, 1936)
Architectural Record (1897, 1904, 1914, 1918, 1926, 1927, 1930)
Architecture and Building News (1894, 1904, 1905, 1908-1914, 1918-1922, 1924, 1927, 1928, 1930, 1931)
Backstage (1976)

Bibliography

Brickbuilder (1908)

Landmarks Preservation Commission (various years)

Marquee (1973, 1976, 1983)

The New York Commercial Advertiser (1911)

The New York Daily News (1982)

The New York Dramatic Mirror (1899, 1900, 1903-1905, 1911)

The New York Herald Tribune (1929, 1932, 1937, 1944)

The New York Mirror (1905)

The New York Morning Telegraph (1941, 1942, 1953)

The New York Star (1917)

The New York Sun (1923, 1925)

The New York Telegraph (1908, 1914, 1927)

The New York Times (1888, 1893, 1900, 1906, 1908-1913, 1918-1920, 1922-1939, 1941-1944, 1952-1960, 1962, 1963, 1965-1970, 1972-1974, 1977, 1979, 1982-1985, 1987-1990)

The New York World (1911)

Pencil Points (1927, 1928)

Playbill (1931, 1952)

Scientific American (1900, 1924)

Stubs (1968)

Theatre Magazine (1901, 1904, 1908, 1909, 1911, 1914, 1915, 1918, 1921)

Variety (1934, 1944, 1972, 1973, 1977, 1981, 1990)

Village Voice (1988)

The Westsider (1977)

Woman's Home Companion (1909)

INDEX OF THEATRE NAMES

Abbey's, 33
ABC-TV, 223
Academy, 195
Adelphi, 243
Aerial Gardens, 73
Alcazar de Paris, 195
American, 29
American Roof Garden, 29
Anco, 87
Apollo, 195
Artef, 113
Assembly, 155
Astor, 101
Avon, 199
Avon-at-the-Hudson
  (43rd Street), 179
Avon-at-the-Hudson
  (44th Street), 67

Belasco, 45
Belmont, 175
Bijou, 171
Billy Rose's Music Hall, 237
Biltmore, 251
Broadway, 19

Candler, 159
Casa Manana, 209
Casino (39th Street), 15
Casino (50th Street), 209
Casino de Paris, 231
CBS Radio Playhouse
  No. 1, 237
CBS Radio Playhouse
  No. 2, 105
CBS Radio Playhouse,
  No. 4, 231
CBS Radio Playhouse,
  No. 5, 109
CBS Studio 50, 237

CBS Studio 51, 109
CBS Studio 52, 231
CBS Studio 62, 251
Center, 247
Central, 183
Central Park, 203
Century, 117
Century Roof, 117
Charles Hopkins, 163
Cinema Dante, 155
Cinema 49, 207
Cinema Verdi, 155
Circle, 53
Coburn, 123
Cohan and Harris, 159
Collier's Comedy, 113
Colonial, 91
Columbia, 183
Comedy, 113
Concert, 223
Cort's 58th Street, 223
Cort's 63rd Street, 123
Cosmopolitan, 57
Craig, 243
Criterion, 37

Daly's 63rd Street, 123
Davenport, 123
D.W. Griffith, 171

Earl Carroll, 209
Ed Sullivan, 237
Edyth Totten, 219
Eltinge, 147
Elysee, 223
Embassy Five, 105
Embassy 49th Street, 163
Empire (40th Street), 23
Empire (42nd Street), 147
Experimental, 123

Federal Music, 231
58th Street, 223
51st Street, 253
54th Street, 243
Filmarte, 223
Fine Arts, 223
44th Street, 151
44th Street Roof
  Garden, 151
49th Street, 207
Folies-Bergere, 137
Ford Center for the
  Performing Arts, 62, 196
Forum 47th Street, 183
Frazee, 87
French Casino, 209
Frolic, 73
Fulton, 137

Gaiety, 105
Gallo Opera House, 231
George Abbott, 243
George M. Cohan's, 129
Gilmore's 63rd Street, 123
Gotham, 183
Gus Edward's Music
  Hall, 53

Hackett, 87
Hammerstein's, 237
Hammerstein's Theatre of
  Varieties, 41
Harkness, 91
Harris, 87
Helen Hayes, 137
Henry Miller's, 179
Hippodrome, 95
Holiday, 183
Hollywood, 253
Hudson, 67

International, 57

Jardin de Paris, 37
Jolson's 59th Street, 203
John Golden, 223

Klaw, 199
Knickerbocker, 33

Labor Stage, 155
Laffmovie, 147
Lew M. Fields, 87
Liberty, 83
Little Met, 155
Loew's American, 29
Lucille LaVerne, 155
Lyric (42nd Street), 61
Lyric (45th Street), 37

Mark Hellinger, 253
Majestic, 57
Manhattan, 237
Manhattan Music Hall, 237
Maxine Elliott's, 109
Mercury, 113
Minsky's Park Music
    Hall, 57
Molly Picon, 203
Morosco, 167
Moulin Rouge, 37
Movieland, 183
Music Hall, 37

Nazimova's 39th
    Street, 127
New, 117
New Amsterdam, 73
New Amsterdam Roof, 73
New Apollo, 195
New Century, 203

New Circle, 53
New Victory, 50
New York, 37
New York Roof Garden, 37
New Yorker, 231
Nora Bayes, 151
Norworth, 175

Odeon, 183
Olympia, 37

Palladium, 231
Paradise Roof Garden, 41
Park, 57
Park Lane, 123
Park-Miller, 179
Playhouse, 135
President, 219
Princess, 155
Punch & Judy, 163

Radiant Center, 243
Recital, 123
Reo, 155
Republic, 45
Ritz, 231
RKO Center, 247
RKO Roxy, 247
Roundabout, 188

Sam H. Harris, 159
Savoy, 67
Selwyn, 187
Shakespeare, 203
Shout, 179
63rd Street Music Hall, 123
Studio 54, 231

39th Street, 127
Times Square, 191

Toho Cinema, 171

Vanderbilt, 177
Venice, 203
Victoria (42nd Street), 41
Victoria (46th Street), 105
Victory, 45
Video Tape Center, 203

Waldorf, 221
Wallack's, 87
Weber & Fields' Music
    Hall, 151
Westminster, 163
Windsor, 143
World, 163

Xenon, 179

Yiddish Art
    (54th Street), 243
Yiddish Art
    (59th Street), 203

Ziegfeld, 227

EPILOGUE

In 1997 fifteen of the fifty-six lost Broadway theatres still survive. The outstanding commitment and determination of The New 42nd Street, Disney, and Livent means that four theatres (the New Victory, the New Amsterdam, the Selwyn, and the Ford Center) will be added to the list of Times Square playhouses offering legitimate entertainment. The Hollywood (better remembered as the Mark Hellinger) and the Biltmore might someday return to the stage, and it is possible that one or two others could once again be open for theatre audiences. But whether or not Broadway needs eight more theatres remains to be seen. Show production has dropped more than 80 percent from its peak in the twenties, often leaving a dozen or more theatres dark at any given time. Theatre booking jams occur periodically, but ease quickly as the economics of the risky business of producing take over. As much as these irreplaceable, landmarked theatres need to be treasured, their preservation must be balanced with the development of alternate uses that can keep them open, inviting, and architecturally intact. The current uses of the Hollywood, Ed Sullivan, and Hudson theatres are winning examples of such creative transformation, as opposed to the planned evisceration of 42nd Street's Harris Theatre. Let us hope that the loss of the great playhouses of Broadway's past leads us to value even more the theatres that will make up Broadway's future.